A VERY UNUSUAL JOURNEY INTO PLAY

Sara Miller McCune founded SAGE Publishing in 1965 to support the dissemination of usable knowledge and educate a global community. SAGE publishes more than 1000 journals and over 800 new books each year, spanning a wide range of subject areas. Our growing selection of library products includes archives, data, case studies and video. SAGE remains majority owned by our founder and after her lifetime will become owned by a charitable trust that secures the company's continued independence.

Los Angeles | London | New Delhi | Singapore | Washington DC | Melbourne

A VERY UNUSUAL JOURNEY INTO PLAY

BEN KINGSTON-HUGHES

SAGE Publications Ltd
1 Oliver's Yard
55 City Road
London EC1Y 1SP

SAGE Publications Inc.
2455 Teller Road
Thousand Oaks, California 91320

SAGE Publications India Pvt Ltd
B 1/I 1 Mohan Cooperative Industrial Area
Mathura Road
New Delhi 110 044

SAGE Publications Asia-Pacific Pte Ltd
3 Church Street
#10-04 Samsung Hub
Singapore 049483

Editor: Delayna Spencer
Senior assistant editor: Catriona McMullen
Production editor: Sarah Sewell
Copyeditor: Clare Weaver
Proofreader: Sharon Cawood
Indexer: Silvia Benvenuto
Marketing manager: Dilhara Attygalle
Cover design: Wendy Scott
Typeset by: C&M Digitals (P), Ltd, Chennai, India
Printed in the UK

Library of Congress Control Number: 2021946446

British Library Cataloguing in Publication data

A catalogue record for this book is available from
the British Library

ISBN 978-1-5297-5346-2
ISBN 978-1-5297-5345-5 (pbk)

At SAGE we take sustainability seriously. Most of our products are printed in the UK using responsibly sourced
papers and boards. When we print overseas we ensure sustainable papers are used as measured by the PREPS
grading system. We undertake an annual audit to monitor our sustainability.

To Karen, for proof-reading, putting up with stuff and being the glue that holds everything together.

TABLE OF CONTENTS

ABOUT THE AUTHOR

Ben Kingston-Hughes is an international keynote speaker, writer and multi award-winning trainer. He is also the Managing Director of Inspired Children and has worked with vulnerable children across the UK for over 30 years. He has appeared on television several times, working on a variety of children's projects, and his distinctive blend of humour, neuroscience and real-life practical experiences have made his training invaluable for anyone working with children. His finest moment though, was when a group of reception children named their class frog after him.

INTRODUCTION

I have now worked with children for over 30 years and in that time have come to a really important realisation. The moments when children are playing have been the most profoundly significant moments I have ever witnessed. I have always known instinctively that play is not merely frivolous but never really been able to fully articulate just how important play is. So that is exactly what this book is about. It is based on years of research and, most importantly, 30 years of working with and observing children. It is full of new stuff, weird and wonderful stuff and just down-right unlikely stuff, all pointing to the inescapable truth that play is one of the most important things we ever do. This is the book I wish I'd had 30 years ago.

I should point out at this point that I have ADHD. I struggle with concentration, unless I become hyper-focused, and I have a very short attention span. I have tried to write this book for people like me. It is dotted with humorous (hopefully) and thought-provoking (definitely) anecdotes of the thousands of children I have worked with. I have hand-picked the "wow" bits of research, the stuff that blows your mind, because this is the stuff my brain remembers. I want this book to be suitable for anyone to read, from the most knowledgeable and well-read, to people like me who only retain facts that are relevant to their life. And this stuff *is* relevant. If you work with children, this may be the most important stuff you ever learn. I have chosen the theories that have underpinned and allowed me to develop the fundamental pedagogy of my whole organisation and the approach I use with some of the UK's most vulnerable children. I have only chosen methods and theories that directly apply to the children I work with and hopefully with your children too.

What is this book?

Obviously, this is a book about play. The book isn't a textbook though. I didn't want to simply reference other people's theories and re-hash what we already know.

I wanted this to be a real book, one that you would actually want to read even if you are not doing an academic course. I wanted it to have comedy and drama and evil magicians, just like my career working with children. I wrote it to inspire and move people to change how they interact with children, and if they then take it further and do their own research and even further training on play, that is fantastic. What I really want though is for people to enjoy and be moved by this book. I didn't want it to read like an academic book. I have mentioned various neuroscientists and theorists but haven't cross-referenced every bit with a specific page in their research. Please feel free to look these people and theories up for yourself. I have also joined the dots where theories combine to create some really interesting links and paint a stunning picture of play. The one thing I haven't done is made stuff up. All of the stories are true and about real children with real and often bizarre outcomes that I have witnessed personally in the last 30 years.

In short, if you are looking for a book to get you through a degree in early childhood studies then this will certainly help but this was not my main aim in writing it. Hopefully, you will read it anyway though, because there is some truly mind-blowing stuff to be discovered about play.

1) Why do children skip? – Play as an evolutionary survival process

Play is an evolutionary survival trait linked to life expectancy. This chapter looks at the fundamental drives of play and how they are directly linked to building strong, healthy adults. We also look at where play sits in the brain and how this manifests in children's behaviour, and at how playing is rewarded with the most potent mix of powerful biochemicals.

2) Stop being a pirate and come and do your homework! – Play as the key criteria for healthy brain growth

Play is a neurological development process that builds the fundamental structure of the brain and underpins all forms of higher learning. Reading, writing and maths are not hardwired into the brain. The fundamental structures for these higher academic tasks are not present at birth but need to be built through experiential brain growth. The process that builds brains is not sitting still, listening to grown-ups speak, but the bits in between – in short, play.

3) Feathers, bald heads and gloopy glue! – Play as the most powerful healing process for children's emotional well–being

Play is a therapeutic discipline with a unique capacity to heal emotional damage through positive biochemistry. In this chapter, we look at the emotional systems in the brain and at how play has a unique emotional and biochemical balancing potential for negative emotions. We look at how negative emotions such as fear, anger and anxiety cause physical damage in the brain and at how play can be used to heal children from that damage.

4) Dragons don't eat peas – Play as what makes us truly human, unlocking imagination and creativity in a way that no other animal on the planet is capable of

Play is the key to unlocking imagination, creativity and complex problem solving. In this chapter, we look at play as going beyond the evolutionary survival process shared with all mammals into the very things that separate us from animals. We look at how play underpins every aspect of a child's imagination and creativity and at how adults sometimes undermine this. We also look at problem solving and divergent thinking and at how play is instrumental in changing our world through the divergent thinkers that have shaped it.

5) Crocodiles, danger and certain death (well, mild bumps and bruises) – The inestimable importance of risky, challenging play

This chapter is all about risky play and how important this is to the development of our children. Do not read this chapter whilst driving or operating heavy machinery.

6) Get that off your head; you'll mess your hair up! – The catastrophic effects of play deprivation

In this chapter, we discuss the bleak state of play for many children today and the catastrophic damage the increase in screen time is potentially doing to children. We discuss the terrifying neurological cost of the decline in play and the crisis in children's mental health.

7) Peow, peow, peow, click – Play as positive behaviour or how to support children to fulfil their play potential

In this chapter, we take a fresh look at the Play Cycle, one of the most genuinely useful theories on play, and how, by combining this theory with current neuroscience, we can begin to understand children's behaviour. We also consider how often play is mistaken for negative behaviour and how knowledge of the neuroscience of play can help us unlock pro-social behaviour in our children.

8) How did you used to play, Grandma? – Play for the future of humanity

In this chapter, we consider how epigenetics impacts on future generations of children and how play may literally transform our species. In this chapter, we look at the new studies in epigenetics that suggest that positive experiences in childhood can alter the DNA of children, allowing benefits to be observed across multiple generations. This is the most mind-blowing research in recent history, with the greatest implications for people working with children and a message of hope for our entire species.

Who is it for?

The primary market for this book is people who work with children. However, as I was writing it, I couldn't help thinking that I wished I had this information when I first became a parent. So, this book is for parents too. Yes, I talk about settings and nurseries but hopefully parents will see that the bits I am talking about are just as appropriate to the home environment. I have tried, where possible, to give specific tips for parents, not because I am a perfect parent (quite the opposite in fact) but because I have seen how useful the methods have been for my own children. The book is also suitable for people working with the older age group. I have had to be careful here. As both an early years worker and a playworker, I have sometimes seen a discrepancy between different views on play between disciplines. I have tried to cater for all ages of children whilst avoiding controversy about what actually constitutes play in the first place. I am using a broad definition of play and playful that includes the sometimes-structured play between a parent and young child and the wild free play of a 7-year-old in their natural habitat (dirt!). I have tried to be faithful to the ethos of Playwork whilst recognising the positive adult interactions necessary for early childhood development. I hope this makes sense but if my cavalier attitude towards definitions of play causes a deep-seated rage then hopefully you can still see the wonderful benefits of play, regardless of your personal definition, and can adapt it to your own setting and age group.

Background

I never set out to work with children. I was kicked off my first degree course for not being very good at handing in work (or attending lectures, etc). I had moved out of my childhood home and was trying to pay the rent with a series of jobs that I kept getting sacked from. I now believe that my ADHD was a barrier to me finding and keeping work because, like many children in school, I find unstimulating tasks agonisingly hard. At this point my mum, who never lost faith in me, suggested I try again at getting a degree via the mature student route. To cut a long story short, I had to pay my way through university, so I turned up for a job interview at an inner-city project working with children. This project worked with children from 2 to 16 years old in an area with a high level of deprivation. I still remember thinking, *"How hard can it be?"*

It turns out it was the hardest work I had ever done in my life but also the most stimulating and rewarding. I was supposed to work there for 6 weeks but ended up working on the project for 13 years.

In hindsight, I now know this job working with children saved me. I may be almost universally rubbish at everything else but working with children showed me I could do a job well for the first time in my life. I shudder to think what would have happened to me if I had not had that job. The funny thing was that even then I did not think of it as my career. I kept thinking that when I got my degree, I would get a proper job. I went on to do an MA and countless other qualifications but somewhere along the way realised, this *is* my proper job. This is the job I will do for the rest of my life. So, I am not just talking in this book about the fact that play is amazing for children but that it can profoundly impact adults too. For me, it saved my life and opened up possibilities beyond my wildest dreams.

So, I don't just work with children now. I manage an entire company of people working with children and I teach a whole range of courses to other people who work with children. I travel the UK and beyond, delivering keynote speeches and training courses on just how amazing play is. I still work with children though and I still see, week in week out, the enormous impact of simple play.

On names

I switch off when I read about child X interacting with child Y, so I have included names in the studies and case studies. Some of these are the real names, where I have permission, but others have been changed. The stories are all real though.

Pictures

I thought it might be nice to ask children to draw a few illustrations for this book. The pictures are from a wide range of ages and abilities, including some with SEND.

On magicians

I may have been a little unkind to magicians in this book. If you are a magician, please don't be offended. I am using magicians to make a point and could just as easily have used balloon modellers or clowns to differentiate what we do when we work with children compared to what a children's entertainer does. I have worked with many magicians in my career and they have not all been evil. One in particular that I have worked with a few times is actually really nice - a brilliant magician and really positive and amazing with children. But every good story needs a baddy!

So, sit back, grab some snacks and begin a very unusual journey into play.

1

WHY DO CHILDREN SKIP? – PLAY AS AN EVOLUTIONARY SURVIVAL PROCESS

A few years ago, I was working in a nursery setting when I witnessed a young child running up to the nursery with his hood over his head, pretending to be Batman. The sheer, joyful exuberance of the child superhero was a wonderful thing to observe. At this point, the child's mum shouted, *"Get that off your head; you'll mess your hair up!"*

At what point did we start prioritising nice hair over play? When did our society forget the wonderful joy of simply being a superhero with a coat hood? Perhaps more importantly, why did that parent not realise that her child was engaged in one of the most powerful developmental processes he would ever experience?

Now, I am not blaming the parent in this example. Very few people truly recognise just how vital play is for our children and, in fact, our society as a whole seems to undervalue play. In order to understand why play is so essential for our children, we first need to ask some very important questions. Some of the questions may seem quite odd but once we understand these simple concepts, we begin to paint the most incredible picture of the power of play.

So, what is play for anyway?

One of the first questions we need to ask when trying to understand play is, *"Why do children skip?"*. OK, so go with this for a moment. Seriously, why do they skip?

When you think about it, walking is the most effective and efficient means of movement for humans. There is an innate drive from birth to get children from the vulnerable, barely being able to move at all stage, through the highly inefficient crawling stage to competently walking. Young children are clearly more vulnerable than adults, so from an evolutionary perspective it makes sense for them to develop the ability to move efficiently as a matter of priority. Anyone working with younger children will see this incredible drive and the intense effort it takes for children to finally learn to walk. Once children are able to walk, they discard crawling as a means of movement because it is woefully inefficient and potentially very slow (try it for yourself some time). Now obviously there are going to be times when walking is not fast enough, so pretty soon children move on to running. Toddlers will exhibit the half run, half "controlled fall" type of movement until they fully master running. So now we have fully developed two modes of movement that are perfectly efficient ways for our bodies to get from A to B. We have discarded all of the less efficient methods of moving (crawling, shuffling on bottom, etc.) and are now complete as a human being. Job done. Why then do most children, without any adult telling them what to do, suddenly begin to skip?

Skipping is far less efficient than running or walking. It takes up more energy per step than walking and cannot approach the speed of running. On the surface, it would seem like an utterly pointless (and quite silly) behaviour, especially as all previous ineffective movements have been abandoned as the child matures. Why would any rational person suddenly start using a pointless and inefficient type of movement? As a developmental step, it makes no sense at all.

Can you imagine any human using skipping to escape from genuine danger?

Figure 1.1   An adult skipping away from a shark, drawn by F

The answer to this question teaches us the first important lesson about play. It would be easy to dismiss the answer as simply, "because it is fun". Whilst this is obviously true, it misses one of the most important points about the role of play.

If you observe a child skipping, you will see that, beyond the big grin on their face, what makes the movement so inefficient is the additional jump on each step. The double jump renders the movement more difficult and consequently less effective. However, that double jump also makes the movement far better at building bone density in the child's limbs. The bone density a child needs for becoming a healthy adult is formed during childhood and so if a child skips (or does other similar silly things) they will have stronger, healthier bones in adult life. This can potentially prevent illnesses such as osteoporosis maybe 40 or 50 years later. Bone density is a key factor in life expectancy and intrinsically important for our adult health.

Skipping is not just about building bones though. The inefficient double jump is also making the cardiovascular and respiratory systems work harder, so the child is building and strengthening the heart and lungs they will need all the way through their adult life. Once again, a strong heart is intrinsically linked to life expectancy. Heart disease is one of the biggest killers in the UK and the healthy heart we need to survive as adults is built in childhood.

A strong respiratory system is the best defence against respiratory illness and airborne viruses and is another crucial aspect of life expectancy. Once again, we build our respiratory system in childhood. There are no second chances and our adult health and even life expectancy depend on the strong, healthy body that we build in our childhood through playful experiences like skipping.

It appears that this seemingly pointless behaviour is giving a child three essential aspects of life expectancy and an increased potential for lifelong physical health.

It cannot be merely a coincidence that children instinctively move in ways that are so counterintuitive and yet so beneficial for their physical development and health. Indeed, when we begin to look at the neuroscience of play, we see that, far from it being a coincidence, it is the fundamental reason for the behaviour in the first place. We also begin to realise that "fun" is not the cause of the skipping but merely a symptom of that wonderful behaviour.

Humans are not the only ones to enjoy play

This brings us nicely on to another question: "If play is frivolous, as many people believe, why do all mammals play?"

So, we all know that mammals play. Anyone who has owned a dog or a cat will tell you that mammals play a lot, often when we least expect or even want them to. This seems like a good time then to introduce the latest addition to my family. I had never owned a dog, nor ever wanted to own a dog, but gradually over the years my resistance has been worn down and so finally last year I agreed to a puppy. For reasons that I won't go into here, we decided to go for a half Border Collie, half Labrador cross-breed, affectionately known as a Borador. According to various websites, Boradors are an ideal family dog combining the playful energy and intelligence of the Collie with the loyal obedience of the Labrador. The websites lied. He is a one dog force of nature, a whirlwind of destruction and quite possibly one of the four horsemen of the apocalypse. Introducing Marley the Borador.

What makes him so challenging? The fact is that he appears to be completely controlled by two very basic drives: the drive to eat everything and the urge to play. When I say he will eat everything, I don't mean *'don't leave that sandwich unattended'*, I mean he will eat the plaster off the walls if you let him. At the time of writing, he has eaten two computer mice, a keyboard, three TV remotes, several shoes, a sleeping bag and a chair. When he is not eating, he wants to play. Every waking minute of every day, he wants to play. Play for Marley involves running, chasing, pulling and shredding. He loves to chase balls or frisbees but won't bring them back to be thrown again. He loves rough and tumble play such as leaping on top of his family and wrestling with them. He loves biting. This last

Figure 1.2   Marley the Borador

one is interesting. It was something that unnerved me at first, having no previous experience of owning dogs. He is not a small dog and appears quite terrifying when he is bearing down on you, preparing to bite you. I initially worried that he was going to hurt a family member but then I realised something. Dogs have a bite force considerably stronger than a human, and even a puppy could bite with enough force to seriously injure us. And yet a Marley bite never breaks the skin. He bites with exactly enough force to apply firm pressure and a healthy dose of slobber.

Tickling rats unlocks the secrets of play?

This links into the work of a really interesting neuroscientist called Jaak Panksepp. Jaak had one of the best nicknames of any scientist ever, which was "The Rat Tickler". He was fascinated by the fundamental drives and emotions that all mammals seem to share. Experimenting with young rats in his laboratory, he observed play behaviours just like our dog Marley, wrestling and tussling, rolling over each other and running about. He then noticed similarities to the play enjoyed by his own children. He found that by tickling his rats he could elicit a positive response just like in his own children. Hence the nickname "The Rat Tickler" because it turns out rats enjoy a good tickle just like children and can even be heard to "giggle" if you listen with a special microphone.

According to Jaak, this behaviour, which is shared with all mammals, throws up another interesting question. The play behaviour itself could potentially make a mammal more vulnerable to predators. The rats who are tussling and wrestling are considerably less attentive to their surroundings and consequently more vulnerable. Why then are play behaviours so universal in all mammals if they pose a clear risk to survival? Our current understanding of evolution is pretty brutal. Behaviours that do not promote survival or, in this case, actively cause vulnerabilities quickly die out. Play as a behaviour has not only persisted over the last 200 million (ish) years that mammals have been on the planet, but has actively thrived. Indeed, in Jaak Panksepp's experiments, rats that played lived longer than rats that did not.

Even more interesting was what happened when Jaak placed a female rat in a cage with two male rats, one of which had had lots of play and the other who had not. The female rat almost always chose the playful rat as a mate, showing that playful behaviours were not only of benefit to the current generation of rats but also desirable as a trait for future generations. In short, playful rats are sexier than non-playful ones! (Who knew?)

Now, as a play specialist this has never seemed to work in my favour but that's a different story. The fact is that all of these observations add up to an incredibly compelling argument for play. Why has play remained ingrained in mammal behaviour over countless generations despite potentially creating short-term vulnerabilities? There is only one answer that fits, only one answer to explain why this odd, frivolous and sometimes silly behaviour is one of the most important behaviours that mammals (including humans) ever take part in. Play *MUST* have an evolutionary survival function that is so powerful it outweighs the short-term vulnerability it creates. Play is a fundamental biological imperative to turn vulnerable young organisms into strong healthy adults. It is an instinctive behaviour that "trains" young mammals in everything they need to survive in a hostile world.

So, when Marley bites us, or shreds yet another tea-towel or chases my children around the garden, he is doing everything he needs in order to train and develop his growing body. He is developing the speed, stamina, balance, cardiovascular system, control and dexterity he needs to survive. When my cats (they are a whole different problem!) race up and down the stairs at 2 a.m., they are training for hunting, evading other predators and finely honing their skills for survival. When a human child kicks a ball, climbs a tree or rolls down a hill, they are doing exactly the same as Jaak Panksepp's rats. They are building the strong, healthy body and brain they need to survive, and just like Jaak's rats this could potentially have a direct effect on their life expectancy.

Now don't get me wrong. I'm not saying that the only function of play is survival. There are, after all, several more chapters in this book where we will discuss other incredible and uniquely human functions of play. But, as a starting point, we need to understand play as a fundamental drive, innate in all mammals to help them survive. It is an essential developmental process, a biological imperative that is intrinsically linked to long-term health and life expectancy. In short, it is a fundamental building block for survival. Once we accept this as the starting point on our journey into play, we begin to see just how catastrophic it is when we restrict this process in our children and how vehemently we need to argue the case for play against those in our society who don't value it. Without being melodramatic, if you have a school lunchtime where skipping, handstands and even in some cases running (I kid you not!) are banned, you are potentially reducing a child's capacity for long-term bone health, heart health and even life expectancy, all in the name of short-term health and safety.

Daisy chains stop play...

There are schools in the UK that have now banned "running" at playtime. I don't mean running with scissors or chainsaws, just simple running. This is restricting a fundamental urge in children that is intrinsically linked to health and well-being. I once worked in a school where they took this to the extreme and actually banned making daisy chains at lunchtime. The Head was convinced that dogs might have potentially urinated on the daisies, causing instant death to all children who touched them. It is a well-known fact that millions of children die every year from "Daisy chain-related death" and if you could spare just £3 a month to help those poor children...

So, where does play sit in the brain?

The fact that Marley already knows the difference between "play" biting and real biting is due to the fact that he has been instinctively practising with those behaviours almost since birth. The key word here is "instinctive". The rats in Jaak's laboratories didn't seem to be consciously aware they were playing (they are rats after all!) – they just seemed to do it. On observing his rats, Jaak was therefore very keen to find out exactly where in the brain that urge to play sits. Now just to be clear, I am not condoning animal testing and I find some of these experiments horrible. However, Jaak further experimented with his playful rats and by surgically disconnecting areas of rats' brains, he determined that play was not in the conscious upper brain but in a much more primitive area called the limbic system.

Figure 1.3   The limbic system

The limbic system is a collection of structures in the mid to lower brain that are responsible for a wide range of functions. Typically, they are involved in instinctive behaviours rather than conscious thought and are responsible for basic emotions and drives such as fear (more of that later) and also long-term memory. The limbic system is sometimes called the Paleomammalian cortex or the "mammal brain" because these structures are shared with all mammals. The urge to play is therefore an instinctive drive in the same part of our brain as other primal drives such as eating, sleeping and sex.

The knowledge of where play sits in the brain has huge significance for anyone working with children and is extremely important when it comes to understanding behaviour. Once again, the word "instinctive" becomes key. Play behaviours are not upper brain, conscious thought-based drives - *"Oh, I see Jessica over there, I must go and play to improve my life expectancy!"*. Play urges are instantaneous, instinctive drives to do whatever seems most developmentally appropriate at any given time. They are also directly influenced by the environment. Different play behaviours are intrinsically linked to the environments that inspire them. This is massively important in terms of how we create enriched play environments for our children. The simplest example is space. If a child is in a large field, their most obvious instinctive play behaviour would be to run. A slight hill might inspire rolling, while a tree or any kind of obstacle would instinctively promote climbing. If you walk past a low wall on your way to nursery, chances are the child will want to walk along that wall to develop their balance. At no point is there too much in the way of conscious thought.

Balance is crucial for survival, so our inner ear needs calibrating in early childhood to ensure we have good balance because without it we would be more susceptible to injuries. What does almost every child do to ensure they develop strong balance? They instinctively spin round until they feel dizzy and fall over. Marley inexplicably spins round with a death grip on his arch nemesis, his tail, for precisely the same reason. Children (and puppies) can afford to practise with balance because they are so much lower to the ground and sustain significantly less (if any) injury from falling. They also have more flexible bones than adults so are ideally suited to doing "practice" movements with a potential for falling because the danger is considerably less. When you are an adult, falling hurts. However, if you have practised falling through play as a child, you are able to mitigate some of that damage because you now know how to fall more safely. All of this from an instinctive behaviour that many adults dismiss as frivolous and often restrict?

Restricting the limbic system

This is the obvious problem. If adults do not see the inestimable value of those instinctive behaviours, they may restrict them. A child will instinctively run in an open space until an adult tells them to slow down. A child will instinctively climb, jump or roll until an adult tells them it is dangerous, or silly or not proper learning, or a hundred other adult reasons to restrict play. A child will instinctively test their limits until an adult tells them they will hurt themselves. The child will learn, but they will learn the adult's limits, not their own.

Finding your own limits and testing your abilities through play

My son as a 4-year-old liked to jump off steps. He would start on the first step and then work his way up. This is a vital risk management technique that allows a child to find their limits and then push those limits as they develop their skill and confidence. When he got to the fifth step, I had serious misgivings about his safety and was about to stop him jumping when I realised that I needed to be very careful how I restricted him in this essential process. I decided to let him attempt one more jump. He jumped off the fifth step, landed, wobbled and then said, "I'll leave it there now" and then wandered off to do something else. Had I stopped him, he would have been working to my limits and have no idea of his own. That one extra jump allowed him to discover his own limits and then move on. Now I know we have to keep the safety of our children as a priority, but we also need to balance their safety with essential development and just use a little common sense. More of this in a later chapter!

A good example of the instinctive nature of play is where a child finds them-selves in a long, thin space – here, their instinct is to run because their limbic system needs them to build their speed, strength, stamina, etc. The problem arises in school because the best long, thin spaces for running just happen to be corridors. If you observe any school corridor for long enough, you will see further proof of the instinctive nature of play. At some point, at least one child (probably several) will do the "run-walk". The "run-walk" is that unique movement when a child attempts to run whilst appearing to walk. This odd, stiff-legged movement is not to be confused with the "walk-run" which is when older adults run at the same speed as walking to give the illusion they are "hurrying"– notably when crossing roads!

This unique movement is a clear indication of conflict in the brain. The limbic system is urging the child to run whilst the upper brain, the more conscious brain, is telling the child that a grown-up has told them not to. The result is an odd movement somewhere in between. Some children are able to resist these limbic system urges and walk in corridors. Others simply can't. There are children who are reprimanded on a daily basis for running in corridors. Some children even become labelled as "badly behaved" for their inability to resist the urge to play. This is not negative behaviour but simply acting on the urges of their limbic system and being thwarted by an adult-based agenda that the millions of years-old limbic system has no concept of.

As a child, I got the cane for running in a corridor. I know this shows how old I am, but I still remember the injustice of it. Being honest, I did run into the deputy head's belly at speed, but it still feels unfair!

Restricting play as a punishment?

One of the ways some schools deal with this kind of behaviour is to set sanctions such as keeping a child in at break. Hopefully, you are beginning to see now how potentially damaging this is. A child who is trying to act on limbic system urges is now being fur-ther restricted by losing the one time when they could potentially act on those urges legitimately. This will not improve a child's behaviour and may be emotionally and developmentally damaging.

I understand the need to stop children running in corridors. I realise that chil-dren need to learn when it is appropriate to act on their limbic system and when it is not, and there are always going to be genuine reasons to restrict chil-dren's play. Running and shouting with joy are wonderful childhood behaviours but not appropriate at a funeral, for instance. The problem is that as a society we seem to have gone too far in restricting these vital instincts. It wouldn't matter that children can't run in a primary school corridor if their lunchtime was a vibrant time of exploration and freedom, with free play being supported rather than restricted. It wouldn't matter that we don't let a 3-year-old climb on the furniture if there was a wide range of other things for them to climb or test themselves on. The truth is that for many children this is no longer the case. Children are stumbling from one adult-based restriction to the next, with the limbic system utterly thwarted for increasingly long periods of time. This is catastrophic for our current generation of children. The times when a child is able to play freely within an enriched environment, where they can freely explore and test their limits, are becoming increasingly less. Correspondingly, those opportunities for building life-long health and even life expectancy have decreased massively for our children, leaving us in a very precarious situation where children are statistically likely to have weaker bones, poorer cardiovascular systems and potentially shorter life expectancy than previous recent generations.

The incredible biochemistry of play

Now we are getting to the most fascinating aspect of that primal, limbic system urge to play. Think about other limbic system drives. Think about food, for instance. Go on, imagine yourself eating your favourite cake or crisps. When you eat a bar of chocolate, or a curry or pizza, it feels good. We don't question it – it just feels good. Why does food feel so good though? Quite simply because eating is a biological imperative that we need to survive. It is an all-consuming drive without which we would die. And the reason it feels so good is because the limbic system rewards us with a huge hit of positive biochemicals that make us feel great. Every similar survival process in the brain is rewarded by a whole cocktail of biochemicals simply to make us repeat that behaviour. And remember that the urge to play is in the same part of the brain as food and sex.

So, what does this mean for our children? It means that when a child plays freely, they are fulfilling a fundamental biological imperative and are being rewarded with the most potent mix of biochemicals. Several potent biochemicals, including benzodiazepines (of which Valium is an example), are produced naturally in a child's brain when they play. This means something really important about play. It means that when our children are running in the corridors, rolling down a hill or a hundred other play experiences, they can become literally stoned on play. This is not meant as a joke or an exaggeration. The biochemicals associated with play contain prescription-grade drugs that actually have a street value. Benzodiazepines are prescribed by doctors for anxiety, so if you were to squeeze children out and bottle those chemicals you could make a fortune selling on the black market. (Please never try this!)

The benefit of that cocktail of biochemicals is inestimable to the emotional well-being of our children, and the problem is that we don't know how many of those chemicals (if any) are produced by sedentary behaviours such as watching screens. At the time of writing, the average screen time for a child in the UK was 7 hours a day. That represents a massive decline in those instinctive play behaviours and a corresponding decrease in the positive biochemicals produced. It is no coincidence that currently the mental heath of our children is also declining.

Play – A powerful all-consuming drive

You would think that the urge to eat would take precedence as a survival trait, but how many times have we all witnessed children "forgetting" to come for lunch because they are so caught up in playing? When Marley steals yet another cushion, even his favourite treats will not coax him to release it because being chased around the garden is more important at that point than food. This anecdotally suggests that in the short term the drive to play is more powerful even than eating when it comes to the future survival of mammalian organisms. Obviously, as children become more hungry, the urge to eat will reassert itself but the all-consuming urge to play is incredibly powerful.

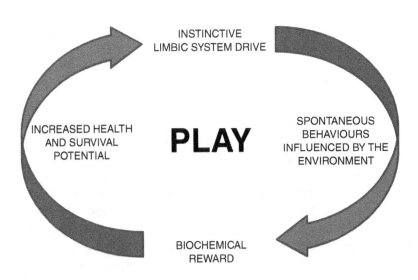

Figure 1.4

So, what does this look like in practice?

First, let's all make a point to prioritise play even more. Its apparently frivolous and unproductive nature means that it sometimes falls between the cracks, especially in the face of learning outcomes and frameworks.

Two fascinating and utterly legendary play theorists, Gordon Sturrock and Perry Else, came up with a range of terminology to describe the process of play (1998). Amongst other useful phrases, they came up with the term "Ludocentric". "Ludo" means play and "centric" means a priority so any setting that takes deliberate steps to prioritise play is following a ludocentric approach.

The ludocentric approach can be profound and life-changing

I have a team of staff who work with vulnerable children across the UK. We work with children that have been through trauma, abuse and bereavement. We use the ludocentric approach as our fundamental pedagogy, not because we believe it is a good way to support those children but because we believe it is the ONLY way to support children who have been through heart-breaking trauma to gain something of their childhood back and begin to heal.

A few years ago, I was working with a group of young children who had been through pretty severe trauma. These were children with very insecure attachments who had experienced a great deal of anxiety in their short lives. I am sure you can imagine the way these children looked at adults. The only way I can describe it is that their faces looked as if they had had such frightening experiences of adults that they were automatically expecting bad things to happen to them. Then we put on masks and superhero capes and ran around the outdoor area. No rules, no adult telling us what to do, just freely chosen joyful movements. The children became fascinated by the way their capes billowed in the wind as they ran. They began to smile and one child even laughed. He then immediately began to cough violently. After we had helped the child, his social worker suggested that he had probably never laughed before. He was experiencing something through play that he had not experienced in any other aspect of his life.

Children need time, space and supportive adults to act freely on their play impulses. Make a point of talking about play at staff meetings and shift the focus from other adult-led agenda. Look at the times when play is restricted and ask ourselves: does it really need to be restricted?

Look at our environment and remember that it will directly influence those instinctive play behaviours. Are our environments enriched (more on that later) and do they offer lots of opportunities for spontaneous play or are they static and uninspiring? Do we have a fantastic hill for rolling down, but children are not allowed to do so (or tree for climbing or puddles for splashing, etc.)? Do we have a wonderful grass area (or school field) but children are not allowed on it for large parts of the year because of health and safety requirements? In short, can our children be children in our environment or are they constantly being told to be something else?

Reflective Question

Do we really need to stop this?

The children in nursery are having a fantastic time making dens and dressing up in old bits of material. Then it is snack time; 11 a.m. is always snack time so surely this is just one of those times when we regrettably have to interrupt play. Once we start prioritising play, however, we realise that maybe play is much more import-ant than the timing of snack and it is perfectly acceptable to occasionally delay it for a while to support positive play.

Look at the instinctive behaviours listed below. Does our environment allow for children to explore these behaviours freely?

- Crawling
- Running
- Climbing
- Jumping
- Balancing
- Spinning
- Rolling
- Manipulating

Does the challenge inherent in those behaviours grow as our children grow? Basically, as our children get older and their abilities are honed, do we provide more advanced opportunities?

Are we as adults modelling those behaviours? Adults are always the most significant influence on a young child's development and well-being. By simply being playful ourselves, we are helping support that incredibly powerful process in children.

Gravity can be tricky!

If you have a hill that children are able to roll down, this is absolutely fantastic for their development and should be encouraged. Why not, once in a while, try rolling up the hill instead? This is a hilarious thing to try and genuinely challenging as you are fighting against gravity the whole time. We randomly tried this with a group of 4-year-olds and they were laughing so hard (especially at the adults doing it!).

Let's stop restricting play as a punishment. Please consider the child's emotional well-being when you are thinking of keeping them in at break or lunch. I have had all sorts of arguments with professionals who insist that keeping children in at break (or recess) is a valid behaviour technique. What it actually does is restrict a fundamental neurological drive that supports children's physical health, emotional well-being and life expectancy, depriving the child of positive biochemicals that help combat anxiety. You wouldn't starve a child who misbehaves, so why would we want to recreate the same biochemical situation by restricting play? As we will see from later chapters, restricting play will also have a huge negative impact on behaviour so the whole concept becomes utterly self-defeating and potentially damaging for children.

Figure 1.5

American states Missouri, Florida, New Jersey and Rhode Island now legally mandate 20 minutes of recess daily for primary age (elementary) children, making it illegal to take away a child's break time, regardless of behaviour.

Crucially, we need to re-look at our current practice with the knowledge that the play drive is essential, instinctive and that we restrict it at our peril. Instead of restricting or limiting play, our priority should be to support and facilitate play. If problems arise due to the limits of our environment, our role is therefore to subtly redirect children's play rather than immediately curtailing those activities that can't take place because of those environmental limits. With the best will in the world, we can't allow children to play in every circumstance in any way their brain wants them to. We are still the adults in this equation and sometimes we are going to have to stop the child climbing the wobbly bookcase because it simply isn't safe. However, if we acknowledge that the climbing child is doing so, not because of negative behaviour or mischief, but because of a fundamental drive to climb then there is a world of difference between saying, *"Mina, stop climbing that bookcase and come and do some colouring!"* and realising that if the limbic system needs to climb, we should be helping Mina to climb by offering an alternative that is at least in the same ball park as climbing a wobbly bookcase!

Reflective Questions – Thinking about play

Think about your children. Do they get plenty of opportunities to explore free play? Do the adults in their life support and enable or restrict and limit? Are there things you could change to enable more opportunities for free play? Even simple things can have an impact, so it is always worth examining current methods to see if there are opportunities for more play. We worked with a school that stopped having a member of staff in the first aid room all lunchtime and instead gave them a portable first aid kit so they could be outside and support play more at lunchtime. Another school purchased huge doormats so the children could play on the field even when it was muddy. One nursery, realising their children loved to dig, provided trowels and actually dedicated a small section of the outdoors for digging holes and finding worms (or *"nakes"* as the children called them).

The most important thing we can do is to reflect on our role as adults. If we acknowledge that supporting play is one of the most important things we will ever do, we can subtly adjust our interactions with children to prioritise play. The way all of my staff are trained is to ask themselves a very simple question when interacting with children, *"Am I making play better?"*

If the answer to this question is "no" then we re-think and come up with something else. If the answer is "yes" then we keep doing what we are doing. It is a simple question that can have a huge impact on our children.

This means that our levels of intervention can be flexible to meet the needs of our children and the situation. Sometimes *"making play better"* is the adult doing nothing at all. When children are fully engaged in play, they don't need an adult. Sometimes it might be providing more resources or even introducing a new idea, if needed, but never at the expense of play. By simply asking ourselves the question, we are better able to support children to work with their brains and play. Nobody gets it right all the time. There have been times when I have "stepped in" when perhaps I shouldn't have. There have also been times when, in hindsight, a positive intervention would have helped children play. However, taking the time to ask ourselves the question, *"Am I making play better?"* means we will get it right a lot more of the time than adults who intervene without taking a moment to consider their impact on children's play.

Note for parents

We are only human. We cannot play with our children all the time and many of us lead very busy lives and are often too exhausted to even think about playing. However, knowing how important play is means maybe we can at least do a little bit more. Maybe we go to the park a little more, maybe we play out in the garden or just turn the TV off once in a while and give our children the time and space to play. It is not always easy, but it is worth it and even a little bit of extra play will help our children.

Finally, what we all need to do is acknowledge the unambiguous benefits of play and stop treating it like an optional extra to children's development. It is easy to say that play is good for children but maybe what we actually need to be saying is that play is profound, essential and life-changing. We need to be loud and proud about play and challenge those who think it frivolous or less important than other agenda. We need to acknowledge play, not merely as an extra value addition to a child's education and development, but as a fundamental foundation for every aspect of a child's journey into adulthood. And, of course, we need to support our children to play because we know that it will profoundly affect their well-being and may even help them to live longer. We need to support play because it is quite literally a matter of life and death.

Chapter Summary

From the work of Jaak Panksepp we know that play is a primal drive seated in the limbic system of our brain shared with all mammals. My own observations of children (and dogs) over the last 30 years have repeatedly supported this, leaving me in no doubt as to how important play is. Play is a biological and evolutionary imperative that is the key mechanism for ensuring vulnerable children grow into strong, healthy adults. It is an instinctive behaviour strongly influenced by the environment that will lead to children intrinsically doing whatever is most developmentally appropriate at any given time and this is regardless of the wishes of adults. Play is rewarded with the most potent mixture of biochemicals, including benzodiazepines that have a profound effect on a child's emotional well-being and make children want to repeat the behaviour.

When we stop children acting on their limbic system through play, we are undermining a fundamental cycle of development that has been evident in mammals for 200 million years and breaking a cycle of biochemical reward that potentially leads to a drop in life expectancy. Remember that the chemicals of play are similar to those associated with eating food so if we constantly restrict children from playing freely, we are doing the biochemical equivalent of starving them.

2

STOP BEING A PIRATE AND COME AND DO YOUR HOMEWORK! – PLAY AS THE KEY CRITERIA FOR HEALTHY BRAIN GROWTH

We now know that play is a fundamental survival process turning vulnerable children into strong, healthy adults. However, this is far from the only developmental benefit of play. The truth is that play underpins all academic learning by being a key catalyst for healthy brain growth.

To understand the unique role of play in neurological development, we need to have a closer look at the child's brain. Without being insulting, baby brains are a ball of mush. At birth, a baby's brain is a fraction of the adult size and has a smooth surface, with a tiny proportion of the connections and physical structure of an adult's. The first six months of life see the most incredibly accelerated brain growth and the first two years are the most critical period for neurological development. This brain growth continues throughout childhood and some areas of our brains are not fully mature until approximately 25 years old.

Why is this significant? Well, the focus in modern society is increasingly towards academic skills such as literacy and mathematics. These concepts seem to be introduced to younger and younger children in an effort to raise levels of academic achievement. Anyone with even a passing knowledge of the architecture of the brain will know this is problematic. The fact is that reading, writing and even speech are not hardwired into the brain. This means that the physical structures to enable those concepts are not built in and are not present at birth. No baby is ever born with the ability to speak, for instance: "*Well mummy, it's been a nightmare 9 months and if Daddy sings that song about an elephant one more time, I'm really going to lose it!...*".

In order to speak, read, write or solve mathematical problems, the child's brain needs to be at a certain level of maturity. In short, a child needs to build the structures associated with all higher academic disciplines before they can reach their full potential. There is even a growing body of research that suggests introducing reading at too young an age can increase the risk of issues such as dyslexia. So surely any education system should be focusing not just on those higher academic disciplines but also on what builds the brain structure to enable those disciplines?

What builds brains?

The truth is that brain growth is not just a natural process that will reach its full potential if left unattended in a dark room. For brain growth to be optimum, certain criteria need to be met. First, brain growth is experiential. This simply means that the brain needs experiences to grow. Crucially, the brain needs a broad range of multi-sensory experiences to grow effectively and one of the key mechanisms for this is play.

Just a cursory investigation into the disparate types of play from sensory play to imaginary play to rough-and-tumble play shows the most incredibly varied experiences, all of which are ideal for brain growth. Sensory play, for instance, is phenomenally neurologically rich and promotes brain growth not just in babies but all the way through childhood. Jaak Panksepp looked at how boisterous play (or rough-and-tumble play) built the frontal lobes of the brain in wrestling rats, and we also know that imaginary play uses a huge neural network and is a powerful brain growth tool. Across every type of play, we see the most incredible potential for brain growth and some of the most neurologically rich experiences a child will ever take part in.

Whilst our upper brain is still growing in early childhood, our limbic system is integrated from birth with hardwired responses and drives such as fear, anger, the need for food and, of course, the urge and drive to play. This means that, from birth, those limbic system motivations are steering a course for brain development, with play being a key mechanism for growth.

You have all heard the classic, *"Daniel, stop being a pirate and come and do your homework!"* and, as a parent, I have even been guilty of similar statements. What we often forget is that being a pirate is potentially building the brain structure Daniel needs to do the homework in the first place.

All work and no play...

Homework is an interesting concept and one that I am firmly opposed to. If we accept the unambiguous evidence that children need a broad range of experiences for healthy brain growth, then why are we making children repeat the same potentially narrow experiences as they have been having all day when they get home from school? In addition, a child who is already disengaged in un-stimulating tasks throughout the school day is not going to benefit from having to complete more of those tasks. Indeed, this could potentially increase their levels of stress and anxiety. Surely, even if there is some nominal improvement in academic ability (and the evidence is far from clear that this is the case) then don't we also need to balance this with the emotional well-being of children?

The fact is that brain growth is, to some extent, on a use it or lose it basis. Neural networks that are activated grow whilst those that are not used do not. The experiences we have in childhood fundamentally change the shape of our brain and current neurological thinking is that experience is more important than genetics when it comes to healthy brain development. No other activity comes close to using as varied and broad a range of neural networks as play. Put simply, nothing else uses as much of the brain as play so nothing else builds the brain in the same way.

Another key criteria for brain growth is human interaction. Even in this we see how vital play is to the process. The playful interactions between parent

and child (or key worker, teacher, playworker and other children) are profoundly important for neurological development. Early games of peekaboo or
simple singing and rhyming are so fundamental to the emotional well-being of
the child that we easily forget that they are also profoundly neurologically rich.

The corpus callosum at work

One area of the brain of note is the corpus callosum. This is a relatively simple
area of the brain that connects our two hemispheres. Basically, it is a cluster
of nerves passing information between the left and right sides of our brain. It
is an essential component in a wide range of tasks such as brain/body control
and it also maintains the flow of information to enable larger neural networks
across both sides of the brain. It is also a key component of stereoscopic vision,
allowing us to process three-dimensional images from two marginally differing
viewpoints (the images from our eyes). One suggestion is that a larger corpus callosum means a greater degree of physical control between the left and right sides
of the body. The corpus callosum is an essential part of the brains of all placental
mammals and begins to develop in the womb. One of the ways it is speculated we
build our corpus callosum is through physical movements that coordinate both
sides of our body. Each limb is effectively controlled by a different side of our
brain so when we coordinate these movements the corpus callosum comes into
play. What do very young children do instinctively through play? They clap. This
simple movement gives audible and sensory feedback and activates the corpus
callosum, creating an early experience of crucial neurological import. How do
children learn to clap? Through the joyful and playful moments of human interaction with their parents or carers as they copy the adult movements and clap
together. Anyone working with very young children will realise that there is also
a short-cut we use for this process. Instead of waiting for the child to copy our
clapping movements, the adult will physically grab the child's hands and make
them clap (usually with a big grin on their face and accompanying silly noises).
This sounds vaguely abusive but is actually a wonderful moment of atunement
play and a unique bonding opportunity between child and adult. It is also hugely
neurologically rich. One of the sad truths about attachment is that a TV screen
cannot grab a child's hands and joyfully clap with them or indeed respond to
a child in any meaningful way. As children get older, they further explore this,
developing whole body movements such as dancing and gymnastics.[1] Even the

---

[1] I am using "gymnastics" to mean the spontaneous exploration of the body's abilities
through energetic movements and "stunts" (handstands, cartwheels, leapfrog, etc.). This
is not the same as "Gymnastics" which is the structured sport or activity as taught by
instructors for the purpose of competition.

humble clap gets an upgrade in becoming complex "pat-a-cake" games requiring ever-increasing dexterity and coordination. It is worth bearing in mind that the ability of a child to coordinate both sides of their brain is an intrinsic element of accurate vision and spatial awareness. As a child scans from left to right, for instance, there will be a movement of activity from one side of the brain to the other. This means that the corpus callosum needs to function to help this process. Why is it important that children can scan from left to right (or indeed right to left) with their eyes? As a basic element of learning to read, a child needs to be able to accurately see what is on the page. Without sufficient brain maturity, this can be a challenge and lead to difficulties with reading which could be problematic throughout a child's academic life. So, does clapping really help children read? An ever-increasing body of research now shows links between early movement and academic skills. Several studies demonstrate how a lack of these movements can negatively impact on learning, including skills such as reading and writing, and one of the many symptoms of impairment of the corpus callosum is speech and language difficulties. When do children make these spontaneous movements? When they are playing.

Play gets children moving

One of the biggest myths about physical activity is that it is predominantly done through sport. Physical activity does not necessarily equal sport and for young children it rarely equates to sport. International children's issues such as increasing obesity levels, low physical activity levels and poor physical health have become epidemic over the last few years. The response of governments seems to be to throw sports coaches at the problem and hope for the best. Don't get me wrong, sport can be incredibly beneficial for both children and adults and there are some amazing success stories about engaging children in sport. However, sport is not the most effective way young children move and potentially disengages a significant number of children. How many of us can remember negative experiences of PE in school and trying to avoid it whenever possible? As the shortest child in our school (pauses for violin music), I spent many a happy PE lesson trying to avoid the ball and doing as little exercise as possible. Once again, we need to go back to Jaak Panksepp to find out the most effective physical activity. Those primal limbic system urges to move existed long before we had organised sport. Instinctive movements, working with the brain through play, do more to engage children in physical activity than any other process. We need to instil a joy in movement rather than a need to compete if we wish to engage children of all ability levels in physical activity. This can only be done through play. Of course, play can be competitive but that is never its prime motivation. In short, play is the key mechanism for physical activity existing long before organised sport.

Early movement essential for brain growth

So, if we accept play as the most powerful catalyst for physical activity, we begin to see enormous neurological implications. The neurobiological effects of physical activity are numerous and impact on a broad range of brain functions. One of the most important effects of regular physical activity for children is increased neuron growth and increased neurological activity. More brain cells that work better! This means that when children are regularly physically active through play, their brains grow faster and operate at increased capacity. This increased capacity has a direct impact on cognition (the ability to understand stuff) which once again has huge implications for academic performance. Another implication is the effect of physical play on working memory, which means that children playing frequently are more likely to retain learning. This is just one of the reasons why, as mentioned earlier, several American states have made recess mandatory for children.

Another myth about development is that it is separated into distinct developmental processes such as the prime areas of the Early Years Foundation Stage. The truth is that to the brain the lines are much more blurred. Early physical development activates overlapping neural networks encompassing parts of the brain associated with a whole range of functions including communication and language. As children, we are never just developing one part of our brain or achieving one specific developmental milestone. Once again, the broad experiences of play enhance and support this development. Imagine a wild and carefree superhero game with a group of 4-year-olds. There is movement of course, balance, coordination and physical strength and speed, but there is also joy, laughter, shouting and noise, imagination and even problem solving as they navigate the space, successfully (or unsuccessfully) avoiding collisions. This is developmentally rich in a way that an organised sports session can rarely approach.

No evidence for play increasing physical activity levels?

One piece of evidence for the universal engagement of children in play comes from a project I worked on several years ago in South Bedfordshire. This was an area of high obesity and low physical activity and NHS funding was available for projects aimed at improving those issues. Several sports initiatives had indicated poor levels of engagement from children and young people. At the time, I was working for a national charity, remote managing a community play project in the area. We had a consistently good turnout of children and what I believed to be very high levels of physical activity. We did not take part in sports on the sessions but promoted freely chosen play activities that focused on the process of enjoyment rather than on a perceived outcome such as winning. In short, we spent two hours messing about, with over 50 children attending every Monday after school. When I enquired as to whether we could get extra funding for our project through the NHS, I was told that there was no evidence to support the fact that free play increased physical activity levels. I decided to conduct a very simple experiment. We bought cheap pedometers and got every child to wear them whilst freely playing on our project. We then got children to wear the pedometers for the same length of time (3 p.m. to 5 p.m.) but on the following day when they weren't attending the project. We then simply compared the results. The average increase in physical activity levels between children playing freely on our project and children following their normal sedentary routine was 992%! Whilst I accept this is a small sample (only 50 children), it did strongly indicate the staggering impact of play on physical activity levels. As a result of this small-scale study, we did receive extra funding from the NHS and continued to impact on the community until all funding ceased and the project eventually had to close.

Too much too soon?

Exploring gross motor skills through play can help children develop fine motor skills. If we want our children to be able to write effectively then one of the best ways to build the required level of brain/body control is to encourage early movement. Remember that a child needs to be at the correct level of brain maturity to be able to have the brain/body control to hold a pen. This maturity may have been delayed by a lack of physical play in early childhood. It may simply be delayed because different children develop at different rates. Regardless of why the child might not be neurologically ready, if on day one of reception class, we are asking all of our children to write their name, some children may find this challenging. This is not to say that these children would not develop the brain/body control given time, but if a child is being asked to do something difficult and even unpleasant then there is a very real danger that the child will make negative associations with literacy. This could be the first step on the road to reluctance that could stay with a child throughout their school life.

Interestingly, one of the finest motor skills a child ever uses is not holding a pen and writing. The intricate movements of the tongue to form words is a fine motor skill that requires extraordinary brain/body control to be successful.

Children who do not have the expected brain and body control for their age are described as having neuromotor immaturity. This just means that they have not moved enough in early childhood, resulting in a series of symptoms affecting the child throughout their childhood and potentially into adulthood. It is no coincidence that in almost every case of neuromotor immaturity there is a corresponding delay in other areas of development including communication and language.

Neuromotor immaturity

Sally Goddard Blythe of the Institute for Neuro-Physiological Psychology has done some amazing work over the last few years in identifying and supporting children who have simply not moved enough in early childhood. She has observed a dramatic increase in cases of "neuromotor immaturity" and in almost every one of these cases there is a corresponding delay in other areas of development, most notably communication and language. This clearly demonstrates that early physical movement is intrinsically linked to cognitive development. Sally then helps children by giving them an intensive programme of movement designed to help the brain/body mature, which has a huge impact on their development and well-being.

It is actually possible to simulate what it feels like for children attempting to write when they don't have the appropriate level of brain/body control. Early years consultant and trainer Kirstine Beeley asks her learners to take off their shoes and socks and attempt to write their name whilst holding the pen with their toes. This is a genuinely challenging experience (and gross if, like me, you are not keen on feet!) and a clear indication of why some children disengage in literacy at a young age. Put simply, if something feels rubbish then children begin to disengage. Disengaging in writing on day one of reception class can be catastrophic for a child's learning potential.

I hate feet!

A seemingly new concept in parks is the bare foot walk. This is where parks or similar establishments create a multi-sensory trail that is designed to be walked bare foot, with children experiencing a range of different textures and surfaces. This is, quite honestly, my idea of hell on earth. I did the bare foot walk at a local country park last year and every single area was just an increasingly soul-destroying new level of foot-based indignity. It was towards the end of the summer season and maybe the trail had not been maintained as well as it should, but it stank, it really stank. The straw was rotten, the mud was stagnant and smelt of a thousand children's feet and the gravel was seriously pointy. Did I mention I hate feet? My wife was literally crying with laughter as she saw me trying to maintain a joyful face in front of my children whilst I silently died inside. This is a fundamental difference between adults and children and one which can lead us to restrict play. Children need those real-life sensory experiences, different textures and yes, different smells (even bad ones) as these experiences help activate neural networks in their growing brains.

How children really learn...

Ironically, one of the least effective ways to build a brain is by sitting still and listening to a grown-up speak. Numerous studies show that learning is enhanced by being stimulating, interactive, physically active or even by taking place outdoors. We all remember those teachers who made their subjects fun. In short, playful lessons are more easily learnt. So, it not just neurological development that is underpinned by play. Put simply, if a lesson in school is playful then children will learn more and will then retain that learning more effectively. If a lesson is static and dull, it is considerably less effective. Added to this are the biochemical responses to play. If a child is engaged in a playful lesson, the chances are they will be enjoying it. If they are enjoying it, they may well be producing a biochemical cocktail including benzodiazepines. This means that positive associations are made in the growing brain, associating the elements of learning with feelings of pleasure.

One of the things everyone seems to forget about learning is that it is a physical change to the structure of the brain. It is not just about filling a database like a computer but actual structural changes to the brain. Because of this, one of the most important things an educator ever needs to know is *"Neurons that excite together, wire together".*

This means that when we create a learning or developmental experience that is playful and stimulating, we don't just activate the parts of the brain associated with learning that particular element but also the parts of the brain associated with positive feelings and biochemicals. And because *"neurons that excite together, wire together",* this creates a neural network associating positivity with learning which is by far the best neurological state for life-long learning. Even more fantastic is that because this is a physical structural change to the brain, over time, if these positive experiences are maintained, the neural network will become hardwired, making it a permanent feature of the brain. From this point on, the child will automatically make positive associations with learning. These are the perfect neurological conditions for a growth mindset.

The opposite of this is where the child makes negative associations with learning – if subjects are dull, fraught with failure thresholds or cause anxiety. Once a child has made negative associations with learning, it is extremely difficult to change their mindset because, over time, this has become a physical, structural change. One common example is maths phobia. If a teacher or other

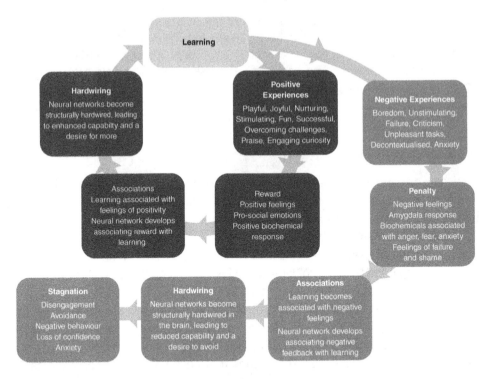

Figure 2.1   The Neuroplasticity of Learning

© Ben Kingston-Hughes

adult induces a child to make negative associations with mathematics by highlighting failures and increasing anxiety, then that child will begin to create negative neural networks associated with mathematics. Eventually, these associations become hardwired so that every time a child encounters maths they will experience the same feelings of anxiety. This does not inspire children to improve, it simply creates a neurological conditioning for anxiety. The child (or adult) will now automatically experience feelings of anxiety at the mere mention of maths. This also intrinsically lowers a child's capability to do maths in the first place, perpetuating the cycle of failure and humiliation. Any sensible person, when faced with an anxious situation, seeks to avoid that situation by any means necessary, so we disengage in maths and seek to avoid it wherever possible.

It is worth saying to any readers who experience anxiety when confronted by maths, please never blame yourself. Adults in your life created this situation when you were a child. It has nothing to do with intelligence or that some people are innately mathematical and others not. It is simply that in your childhood neural networks were created in your brain that automatically associate maths with anxiety.

One way to combat maths phobia is to make maths much more playful so that a child experiences the positive biochemicals of play helping overcome the biochemicals associated with anxiety. This can, over time, slowly re-wire the brain for positivity and hardwire associations of positivity with maths.

But weren't we talking about brain growth?

OK, back to brain growth. There are several criteria for healthy brain growth. Chief among them are enriched environments (i.e. lots of things to play) and positive interactions (i.e. someone to play with). We will be spending a whole chapter later in the book looking at just how profound those enriched human and physical environments are for the neurological growth of children. However, there are also biological criteria that need to be met. A biochemical called Brain Derived Neurotrophic Factor (BDNF) is essential for the growth and maintenance of brain cells. This complex protein plays a significant role in neurogenesis (new brain growth).

It is also an interesting example of how biochemicals are named. Brain derived = made in the brain, Neurotrophic = brain growing, Factor = erm, stuff? So, the literal translation is "made in the brain, brain-growing stuff". This chemical is basically a fertiliser for the brain: the equivalent of Baby Bio for growing healthy brain cells.

As to why this is important, we need to go back to our old friends, the rats. In experiments with rats, it has been shown that when engaging in play there is an increased level of BDNF production. This means that not only are the environmental criteria for healthy brain growth met through play, but also the biochemical conditions through the production of BDNF. Interestingly, increased BDNF production was also noted when rats were encouraged to explore their environment, which suggests that curiosity also plays a part in the production of this fascinating hormone.

OK. so what does this look like in practice?

Once again, we need to prioritise play and understand that the blueprint for neurological development is already there waiting to be unleashed. We need to be looking at all of those instinctive movements and actions and making sure that children have the time, space and emotional security to work with their brain.

There is a tendency in many childcare and educational establishments to differentiate between times of play and times of learning. The thinking being that the play times help children let off steam so that they are ready to learn during the more important learning times. In this scenario, when more

Figure 2.2 Brain Derived Neurotrophic Factor - Fertilizer for the brain!

learning needs to be achieved then the level of play time can be reduced to make time for the truly important business of learning. There is also the tendency to give less worth to play when compared with other agenda. So, for instance, less value is often assigned to digging a hole outdoors than learning numbers or letters.

The truth is that play is not separate from learning but is the most effective form of learning as well as being hugely significant for brain growth. For any establishment to be truly effective at embedding life-long learning, there should be no differentiation between play and learning, and opportunities for play should be embedded throughout every aspect of the daily routine. What we really need is a paradigm shift where instead of looking for ways to integrate more play into the formal learning programme of a setting, we should be seeking to playfully integrate formal learning into the truly important business of play.

Kung Fu Phonics (HI YAH!)

The amazing phonics specialist Anna Lucas makes her phonics so incredibly playful through singing, dancing and kung fu moves that children would never identify this as anything other than play. This is one way in which we can seamlessly integrate more formal learning into play.

Children digging holes is a wonderful, neurologically rich experience in its own right and does not need any educational remit forced upon it. Children are already learning mathematical concepts such as area and volume as well as problem solving and activating huge areas of their brain through physical activity. In a play setting, this requires little or no intervention and is a complete experience for children. If, however, an educational setting wishes to expand on this, then instead of "stopping" the play they can seamlessly move into more structured (but equally playful) explorations of mathematical concepts of volume, for instance. Rather than stopping play to come and do some maths, we make maths as joyful, active and playful as possible, meaning that there is no jarring transition between "modes" of experience and we maintain the perfect biochemical balance for learning as well as optimising opportunities for brain growth. This fundamental understanding that play is the route of successful learning turns the established order on its head but is a profoundly valuable pedagogy and when used effectively is truly transformative for children. The ludocentric approach is therefore not merely about well-being but can be a powerful learning pedagogy. I understand how this could sound controversial to Playwork settings, so, to clarify, I am not suggesting that a Playwork setting should ever have an educational remit. What I am suggesting is that settings where education is mandated by curriculum make learning more playful and integrate with times of free playful exploration.

Manky parsnip anyone?

I recently visited a ludocentric setting in the Midlands and had a fantastic afternoon working with some incredibly imaginative and creative children. Like many settings, they used real fruit and vegetables instead of plastic versions to give a broader range of sensory experiences. Also like many settings, the fruit and vegetables were a little past their best after being handled by the children for a few days. Whilst a majority of the children were busy interacting with each other, making increasingly ambitious dens out of cardboard, one young child was playing by herself. She had found a grubby, wrinkled-looking parsnip and some string, and was meticulously wrapping the string around the parsnip. In some establishments, this behaviour could have been seen as unproductive and many people would have stopped this or made her join in with the other children: "Stop playing with that manky parsnip and come and do something fun!" However, in this setting the child was able to explore her playful curiosity and play how her brain urged her to. Far from being unproductive, this was an extremely powerful exercise in coordination, fine motor skills and concentration. She was also using a pincer grip on the string which is an intrinsic skill in holding a pen. No practitioners stopped her but one stepped closer and just made a few surreptitious notes about the learning and development to record later. If a well-meaning adult had stopped this wonderful activity, all of that learning would have been lost.

For older children, we need to understand that their brains may well be starved (literally) of play when they arrive at our setting. In order for children to have the broadest range of experience and therefore the greatest potential for brain growth, we need to make sure that our afterschool club, for instance, is as vibrant and playful as possible rather than just a continuation of school. In school, we need to recognise that children's play has declined at home over recent years and so moments of free play have become even more precious. We need to make sure our lunchtime is an oasis of free play, giving children vital time to emotionally reset and to enhance brain growth through their enriched experiences. We need to re-examine our approach to formal learning and look for opportunities to make things more playful. Remember that negative experiences of learning change the fundamental structure of the brain and can create a life-long disengagement. The only way to overcome this is to make learning more playful and fun.

Embedding play throughout every aspect of the daily routine of the setting is an intrinsic part of the ludocentric approach. It is also extremely powerful in terms of physical activity levels. Current UK guidelines are for children to have a prescribed level of daily physical activity so, for instance, toddlers and pre-schoolers should have 180 minutes with the stipulation that "more is better". If we accept the unambiguous neurological benefits of physical movement then embedding physical play throughout the day can be profoundly important for our children. Rather than parcelling up the day into times of physical activity and times of being sedentary, make physical activity a central part of the day. Make transitions between different areas playful and active. Follow the leader to go to where we have our lunch or make sure we dance when moving between indoors and outdoors. Simply having key workers, teachers and other adults who are modelling playful behaviours will give inspiration and, crucially, permission for children to move more freely and confidently in our setting.

Enter the magician (pause for evil laughter)

On one of my projects working with vulnerable children the organisers had also hired a magician. This on the surface seems innocent enough but that's just what the magicians want you to think. All the way through the session, my staff team were creating the most wonderful free play opportunities for the children. At almost every turn, the magician would undermine these by walking up to a fully engaged child and saying things like "pick a card" or "pull my finger". It was a frustrating day for my team because we wanted the children to be able to explore freely and play how their brains needed them to. The magician kept undermining that process. The magician had been hired to perform and that meant that he always had to be the centre of attention, constantly making children look at him and engaging them with a series of tricks. It didn't help that he was dressed in a giant chicken outfit. Now don't get me wrong, some of the tricks were really good, and there is definitely room in children's lives for a magician or two. Unfortunately, the manager in charge of our team (not me) had finally had enough of these interruptions and mindful of his role to support play, may have made a few comments to the magician (definitely wasn't me). Also, unfortunately, this manager was socially inept when talking to adults (still not me) so may not have handled the situation particularly well and ended up upsetting the magician. Whilst in the carpark, the magician then threatened me (I mean the other, unrelated manager) with actual violence which was only slightly undermined by the fact that he still had his giant chicken costume on. The saddest fact of all is that this was not the first time I had been threatened by a magician (or a chicken). OK, it was me - I did it, I offended a magician - are you happy now?

Now, I am not anti-magician, but this really illustrates the difference between what we were doing and what children's entertainers do. For us, supporting play is not about entertaining children but about facilitating the way for children to entertain themselves. Play is always something children do and very rarely something that is done to them. That is not to say we don't entertain children, it just means our focus is not on us but on them.

Figure 2.3 Evil Magician drawn by K

Adulteration

Another term coined by Gordon Sturrock and Perry Else (1998) is adulteration. Adulteration is where adults deliberately or unconsciously undermine or restrict play. This is not to be confused with adultery, which is something completely different!

Adulteration can happen for many reasons, but health and safety is a key one and the mistaken belief that play is frivolous is another. Maybe it is the vain belief that anybody cares which card you have picked (it was the 3 of Clubs, OK?). The ludocentric setting seeks to minimise adulteration by supporting children to play freely as much as possible and removing restricting influences. Of course, there are going to be times when we restrict play through necessity, home time for example, but once again we seem to have gone too far and as a society we are adulterating more than is healthy for our children. Adult agenda often seem to take precedence over play and sometimes it seems that children are constantly being stopped from playing because it is noisy, messy, overly boisterous, etc. The ludocentric setting supports play by taking that moment to think about whether it is really necessary to restrict it, and on the occasions when it does become necessary, attempts to find alternatives rather than completely stopping play.

It shouldn't be used for that!

One way in which we adulterate is by having a very narrow view of how resources should be used. In one nursery, a young boy climbed into the baby's Moses basket and began to row and sing the obligatory *"row, row your boat"*. The key worker was overheard to say, *"Joshua, get out of there, that's for the babies!"* Luckily in this instance, one of my managers was present and simply asked the key worker, *"When was the last time you heard Joshua sing?"* Joshua was a very quiet child who rarely joined in with group singing time. She then asked, *"When was the last time you saw Joshua so engaged in an activity?"* Joshua was a very underconfident child whose levels of engagement were often low. The fact was that Joshua was working with his brain and fully engaged in play. He was achieving a unique level of development that should not have been stopped simply because it did not conform with the adults' view of how the Moses basket should have been used. Sometimes taking that additional moment of thought is all it takes to significantly increase opportunities for play and avoid adulteration. Now I am not saying that we let children do anything they want. We need to use common sense and if Joshua was damaging the Moses basket so that other children would not be able to use it then of course we would stop him. However, we would then try to find a similar opportunity for Joshua to explore through play.

So, the ludocentric approach is not about always letting children do anything they want but about prioritising play and enabling that free exploration so valuable for experiential brain growth. When there is a genuine need to adulterate, it is about steering a child towards a positive expression of their play urges rather than restricting play altogether. It is about having an open mind about resources. Let's be honest, a cardboard box was never designed for children to sit in, and yet this is the first thing they will instinctively do. Pots and pans were not designed as drums but make an excellent, if annoying, substitute. Once we start limiting a child's ability to see multiple uses for objects and restrict them to merely what they were designed for, we undermine a fundamental creative process of huge significance to the development of the child. More of this in later chapters!

By simply observing children, I have witnessed a significant difference between approaches across thousands of nurseries, schools and afterschool provisions. When settings are overly structured, restrict play or have adults who are simply not fun, there is a very real danger that some children will be anxious, underconfident and less engaged. The settings that encourage free play, exploration and experimentation with interesting resources, and crucially have playful staff, show the most marked difference in the children in their care. I have visited settings where the enthusiasm and joy of the children is palpable as you walk in the door. They are vibrant, creative, sometimes mischievous, and above all happy (and that's just the staff!). I cannot stress how obvious this difference is to an outside observer. Not only is the ludocentric approach helping children thrive emotionally, it is also creating the optimal conditions for healthy brain growth and giving the broadest range of playful experiences.

Standing up for play!

A few years ago, I designed an intensive training course to help adults understand and advocate for play. This course is called the Play Champions Award and is one of my favourite courses to deliver. One of my Play Champion students was also a lunchtime supervisor in a primary school. In this school, the reception class (5-year-olds) were not allowed on the grass at lunchtime because the older children were playing. Instead, they had a small concrete area surrounded by bars. Play will find a way though and some of the children were reaching under the bars to pull grass so they could make nests for ladybirds. This is creative, innovative, natural play and the perfect neurological conditions for brain growth! That is until another lunchtime supervisor blew her whistle at the children and told them to stop picking the grass. The Play Champion marched up to the other supervisor, blew her whistle at her and shouted, "LET THOSE CHILDREN PLAY!". Earlier that day on the training course, I had been explaining to the Play Champions all about "adulteration" and that our role was not just to facilitate play but also to stand up for children's rights to play against people who restrict it.

Reflective Questions

Think about your children and the experiences they have in your care. Think about ways you can broaden their range of play experiences to maximise the potential for brain growth. Remember that in early years, broadening experiences is also directly linked to cultural capital and future aspirations.

What types of play do your children enjoy? How can we introduce new experiences and extend play? Are there ways you can make formal learning more playful?

Think about levels of physical activity in your children. Put simply, do they move enough? How can we incorporate more joyful, playful movements into children's lives? Look at your own practice. Are you joyful, playful and fun with your children? Remember that you don't have to feel fun on the inside (bare foot walk anybody?) to be fun on the outside!

Most importantly, think about adulteration. Are there times when we can avoid adulteration and simply let children play? Do we have colleagues or staff members who maybe restrict play too much?

During one school lunchtime, a child was lying on the floor looking at clouds. One midday supervisor told him to get up off the floor and stop being silly. Another lay down next to him and spent several minutes talking about the shapes and creatures they could see. Sometimes the most powerful thing you can do for children is to be a different sort of grown-up.

Chapter Summary

Brain growth is experiential, requiring a wide range of experiences to reach its full potential. Play gives children the broadest range of experiences, activating the largest areas of the brain and making it one of the most important criteria for healthy brain growth. Reading, writing and maths are not hardwired into the brain but need levels of brain maturity to be effective. A crucial way to build this infrastructure of the brain is through play. Physical play in early childhood underpins a whole range of developmental processes, including communication and language, literacy and mathematics. In addition, play increases levels of brain growth hormones, speeding up and optimising brain growth and health.

3

FEATHERS, BALD HEADS AND GLOOPY GLUE! – PLAY AS THE MOST POWERFUL HEALING PROCESS FOR CHILDREN'S EMOTIONAL WELL-BEING

In this chapter, we are looking at one of the most important aspects of play and one which I have seen first-hand over 30 years of working with children. Many of the children I have worked with would be described as "vulnerable". This can be for a variety of reasons. Some of our children have experienced abuse, neglect or bereavement. Others have special educational needs or disabilities, or behavioural issues, and some of our children are struggling with mental health issues such as anxiety. The one thing that all these children of different ages, social backgrounds and needs, have in common, is the unique power of play to help them heal emotional damage. So, in this chapter, we are looking at the unique therapeutic properties of play.

In my career, I have worked alongside numerous therapists and other wonderful professionals who use play as a method of supporting emotional well-being. In my work, however, the primary focus has never been about therapy. I have not sought to use play as therapy but through play have seen the most incredible therapeutic benefits. This may seem like a subtle distinction, but it is important to understanding this unique function. It sounds like a cliché but in most of my sessions the goal is just to enable vulnerable children, through play, to simply be children again. The fact that through these moments of play they reap the most profound emotional benefits is not a coincidence but is never our primary motivation.

Why then the distinction? Simply because in this chapter I am not talking about deliberate interventions using play to help children who have been through emotional trauma. I am talking about moments of freely chosen play that have a profound impact on children. Play used as therapy is amazingly powerful as a targeted approach, but the truth is that play is a fundamental process in its own right. This does not mean that I am dismissing structured therapeutic disciplines, far from it, just that by focusing on play in its broader sense we can help children heal as part of an entire spectrum of benefits.

One of my staff occasionally dresses up in a skin-tight yellow body suit with matching mask and cape and becomes "Banana Lady". In any other environment, people would probably consider her appearance ridiculous. However, twice in our sessions, selectively mute children have been able to talk to "Banana Lady" when they will not talk to any other adult. She does not dress up with the intention of helping children speak, but through her "playfulness" and the superhero games she plays with the children, they become emotionally secure enough to be able to communicate more effectively. Far from ridiculous, she is one of the best practitioners I have ever worked with.

Saving mermaids!

A few years ago, I worked with a young boy called Michael who was extremely anxious and had a very noticeable stammer. His home life was appalling and he was extremely vulnerable. During one session, we made ships out of cardboard boxes and spent the entire time pretending we were pirates, complete with home-made costumes. I will never forget Michael standing in the prow of his ship shouting, *"Let's save the mermaids, lads!"*. There was not even the barest hint of a stammer in his voice as he confidently led his gang of pirates.

This is something I have witnessed on numerous occasions. There seems to be a moment during play where the anxiety of the world finally loses its hold and children are able to play freely. Many things can trigger this moment. Sometimes it takes only minutes, for other children it can be months. For some of our children, simply sitting in a den or a cardboard box can create that moment of emotional well-being. For others, it has been overcoming challenges such as climbing trees or attempting stunts. For some it involves laughter, for others intense concentration. The one thing all of these things have in common is that in every case the children are supported by positive, playful adults.

I recently met a young man who it turned out I had worked with many years ago when he was a child. I knew at the time that he came from a very challenging home environment. I also knew that all of his older siblings had ended up either in young offender institutes or in prison. He hated school and from day one felt he had been treated badly because of the previous behaviour of his older siblings. He introduced me to his wife and baby daughter and told his wife that our project was the reason he didn't end up in prison. He said it was the only place he had felt at home growing up.

Emotional systems in the brain

The fact that I have observed so many wonderful moments where children's emotional well-being has been profoundly improved through play cannot be merely coincidence. In order to understand why, time and time again, those moments of play have led to a breakthrough, we need to go back to our old friend Jaak Panksepp.

Jaak did not just look at play in the brain, he also looked at our other primal drives and emotions. He proposed a whole series of emotions hardwired at birth and influencing our behaviour throughout our lives. I mentioned briefly the desire for food and sex but there are other emotions equally important to our survival but very different in how they affect our behaviour. In order to understand how play can change children's lives, we need to first look at some of our darker emotions and, in particular, anger, fear and anxiety. These three emotions are sometimes called the alarm systems because they trigger an "alarm" in our brain that gives us a response to danger. The alarm in our brain is called our amygdala and to explore the impact of these emotions fully we need to go on a journey into this fascinating and terrifying part of the brain.

The amygdalae are almond-shaped structures in the limbic system of the brain. Shared with all mammals, they are responsible for a whole range of functions including processing memory of emotional events. One of the primary roles, however, is processing danger responses such as anger, fear and aggression. Put simply, the amygdala is a primitive part of the brain, processing responses to dangerous situations and helping us avoid or escape those situations. As with much of the limbic system, the amygdala has an evolutionary survival function to make sure we survive into adulthood and pass on our genes to the next generation.

One thing we need to understand is that the amygdala is 200,000 years old (ish) in humans but shared with all mammals, so potentially 200 million years old. It is in our brains to protect us from threats, giving us appropriate responses to danger and potentially saving our lives. The trouble is that the amygdala has not changed for so long that our responses to threats are no longer always appropriate.

As an example, let's examine maths phobia once again. Experiencing maths causes fear. Fear activates the amygdala, giving a range of responses to escape the perceived danger. However, the amygdala is geared up to protect us from primitive dangers that existed millions of years ago. So, when the teacher asks a maths-phobic child what 6 times 12 is, a part of the brain is activated that is protecting the child from a cave bear attack. The traditional responses of fight, flight or freeze may be effective against a cave bear but are pretty useless when it comes to fear of maths. We can't fight the maths (or the maths teacher!), we can't run away from the maths and we can't lie still so the maths thinks we are dead and leaves us alone. Essentially, we are stuck with these powerful, primitive instincts in a situation in which they have no place or effect. Therefore, if a child experiences anger, fear or anxiety, they are essentially reacting to a primitive threat regardless of what has actually caused those feelings. They will consequently become more aggressive (and pre-disposed to negative behaviour) as a defence against the primitive threat.

The catastrophic effect of fear and anxiety

So, what actually happens when a child is scared (or angry or anxious)? One of the first things to occur is that the child becomes less intelligent. This may seem an odd thing, but it is actually something we have all experienced. Even as adults, when we are put on the spot or feeling anxious, we can actually forget information we previously knew and make mistakes that simply wouldn't have happened if we were feeling calm. I don't know about you, but I dread the moment on training courses when the trainer asks us to go around the room and everyone say their names and a bit about themselves. For me, it is like the circle of death, waiting for my turn and then invariably messing up, forgetting my name and losing the ability to speak in coherent sentences or even understand what other people are saying.

Real man?

I will never forget that after working on a children's project in Rochdale I came face to face with an irate lorry driver because I had accidently blocked his lorry in with our company van. I became instantly more anxious, deepened my voice (in a vain attempt to appear more manly) and was about to call him *"mate"* when my brain froze in panic. *What if the word "mate" makes him even more angry?* In a split second, my panicking brain decided to supply another word instead. I heard my self say, as if from a distance, the words, *"Sorry chappy!"* There followed a long and very awkward silence. I have never used the word "chappy" in my life and yet in that moment of panic my rational brain was not operating at full capacity. The reason is simple: fear impairs thinking.

The reason behind this is fascinating. One theory suggests that this lowering of intelligence is yet another evolutionary survival trait. The capacity of the human brain for rational, conscious thought could potentially come into conflict with the primal instinctive drive to escape danger. Animals will always react instinctively to danger. If a cat or dog sees a threat, they will react instantly and with no conscious thought. (Imagine Scooby Doo running at this point - *Yoiks!*)

Put simply, a cat cannot do a parachute jump. Whilst a human can, to some extent, override their amygdala with conscious thought: *"It's for charity"* or *"It will be an amazing experience"*, the cat can't do this. However, the more scared we become, the less able we are to do this as our upper conscious thinking brain is cut out of the equation.

Figure 3.1   Parachuting Cat drawn by R

Skydiving cats

Interestingly, I googled "cats doing parachute jumps" to see if there was a funny clip art image and to my shock found a news article about a cat that actually does parachute jumps, thus disproving everything I have just said. However, on examining the article, it turns out that the cat is doing a tandem jump with his owner who literally straps the cat to him before he (not the cat) does a parachute jump. This is not a cat overriding their amygdala, merely a human traumatising a cat.

"Animal instinct" means just that, completely controlled by limbic system drives to avoid an immediate danger. Humans are different though. We have a much more self-aware upper brain that allows us to think. It is obviously of huge benefit to our species but in certain circumstances could potentially put us in harm's way: *"Oh, is that a cave bear coming towards me? What interesting fur it has, I wonder if it will be friendly urk!......"*

To avoid overthinking dangerous situations, the amygdala responses trigger a shutting down of higher cognitive thought to ensure we act on instinct to avoid the immediate threat. This disconnection of cognitive function is progressive and so the more frightened or angry we become, the less capable we are of conscious thought. We have all said and done immature or thoughtless things we later regret when we are in the throws of anger, for instance. This is because our moral code or sense of right and wrong and feelings of empathy are believed to be in our upper brain so are progressively impaired by fear, anger and anxiety.

So, back to our maths-phobic child. If we ask the child a maths question that makes them anxious, they are then progressively less able to answer the question that caused the anxiety in the first place. Sadly, this progression can lead to a child who is so scared they are barely operating on a conscious level and completely acting on their amygdala system responses. They are unable to express themselves effectively and unable to understand any new concepts.

Negative behaviour?

I worked with a school a few years ago and was being shown around by the Deputy head. Whilst walking down the corridor, I saw a group of children waiting to go into the class-room. Someone had accidently left a box of multi-coloured torches in the corridor and so without conscious thought the boy nearest to them began to reach for a torch. A class-room assistant saw him and loudly shouted next to the child, *"We've got one here playing with torches."* The class teacher strode down the line of children and started shouting at the same boy for not lining up properly. *"I've had enough of your behaviour, Byron...."* At this point, the Deputy joined in and also began haranguing the child about his behaviour. The child had his back to the wall whilst three adults shouted at him and within twenty seconds his lip was curling and he was snarling and spitting. Those three professional adults had frightened and enraged a child to such an extent that he was incapable of anything except the most primitive of behaviours. They then proceeded to chastise him for his attitude and at that point I had no alternative but to step in. I picked up a torch and said, *"Excuse me? I've touched a torch - are you going to talk to me like that?"* There was utter shock on their faces at being challenged, but the saddest thing was that they had not even considered the fact that how they were treating that child was abusive. They clearly thought it was a perfectly acceptable way to deal with so-called "negative" behaviour. I was sickened by the experience and can only guess at the damage they were doing to their children. The truth is that it wouldn't have mattered how much they tried to explain Byron's behaviour to him. At that point, Byron was effectively no longer present to the extent that he could no longer understand what was being said to him. What they had created was a child so caught up in his amygdala responses and so devoid of higher cognitive thought that any discussion of behaviour was pointless. He was, to all intents and purposes, an animal version of himself.

Amygdala responses lower intelligence and increase aggression, two behaviours that are not particularly helpful for a child in school or nursery. If a setting regularly makes children feel anxious then their capacity to learn will be impaired. If a child comes from a home environment where they frequently feel anxious or afraid then they will be pre-disposed towards negative behaviour and aggression. Even the stressful school or nursery run, that as parents we have all experienced, can impact on our children: *"Come on children, we're late, what do you mean you've lost your shoes? You just had them on. Don't do that to your sister! Now the dog has been sick! ...."* Our children now arrive at school or nursery in a less than optimum state for learning or behaviour because of the stress levels they have experienced. Hopefully though, the school or nursery are welcoming and emotionally secure places where our children can soon calm down. However, this is not always the case, especially if the child is exhibiting negative behaviour.

Stress is toxic (literally!)

Unfortunately, the lowering of cognitive function is not the only negative aspect of amygdala activity. Just like food and sex (and of course play) there is a corresponding biochemical response. This biochemical response is not, however, a positive feeling to make you repeat the behaviour but a series of chemicals to help us avoid danger. Stress hormones such as cortisol are produced whenever we experience anger, fear or anxiety. The purpose of these chemicals is to increase our survival chances in dangerous situations. They serve a vital survival function and, when no longer needed, safely leave our system with negligible harm done.

However, research suggests that excessive amounts of these chemicals are toxic. This is not a problem if the child is subsequently able to feel safe, calm down and stop producing the chemicals. The problem is that if a child is made to feel anxious, angry or afraid, this will impair their ability to learn and increase the chances of negative behaviour. They will not do as well at academic tasks and may feel humiliated, leading to more anger and fear. This unfortunately can make adults much more likely to continue to treat the child negatively, further increasing the production of stress hormones.

If the child has no opportunities for respite from the stress-inducing factors, then these chemicals will remain present in increasing amounts. In addition to being toxic, these chemicals are acidic and can cause burning to areas of the brain which further impairs learning, development and behaviour. Long-term exposure to cortisol also leads to damage in the hippocampus (another region of the limbic system) which impairs learning even more. This means that anxiety, fear and anger are not merely "bad" for children but, if left unchecked, can cause actual physical damage to their brain, with potentially catastrophic results for their long-term well-being.

When cortisol is injected into animals (our old friends the poor rats again), they exhibit signs of depression, anxiety, aggression, increases in heart rate, disrupted digestion, decreased appetite, disruption of sleep, suppression of exploratory activity, startle responses and freezing and fighting behaviour. In addition, excessive cortisol can supress our immune system, making it ideal as a medicine to reduce inflammation but with serious long-term health issues for people experiencing excessive stress. In short, stress is biochemically bad for all of us but is particularly catastrophic for children because it can create a cycle of impaired learning and negative behaviour than can be very difficult for the child to see a way out of.

A parent's story

My son really struggled in primary school. In year 4 he had a teacher who had a reputation for being unpleasant and strict. Other parents reassured us though, saying things like, "She's a bit mean but he's only got her for a year and the next teacher is really nice." Six months later, my son actually stopped eating because he was so frightened of this teacher. He stills struggles with school anxiety five years on and we were forced to remove him from that school altogether. At the time I kept thinking, "I had strict teachers when I was young and it never did me any harm." This is the biggest myth about teaching. Mean adults harm children. The degree of that harm is influenced by a multitude of other factors, but the truth remains that this style of teaching damages children and should have no place in modern education. Simply examining the biochemistry of the situation shows us how potentially damaging this is for children. My son would have already been in a state of heightened stress before even entering the classroom due to his fear of this teacher. This state made him biochemically impaired from learning at his full potential. He then had no respite (yes, he was sometimes kept in at break!) and subsequently spent the whole day with his brain awash with toxic biochemicals, further impairing his capacity to learn and severely damaging his confidence, self-esteem and emotional well-being. Understandably, his behaviour deteriorated at home too. I finally realised how serious the problem was when I took him to school and he refused to go into the classroom because he had not finished his homework. I said I would go in with him and explain things to the teacher and he looked at me in panic and said, "Don't! She'll tell you off too!" He was so frightened of his teacher he was trying to protect me from her. I strode into the classroom spoiling for an argument only to be greeted by the classroom assistant. She clearly knew something was wrong because before I could speak, she said, "Don't worry, she's not in today." The six nearest children cheered at this news. The truth is we never know fully how much damage negative adults can cause but in my son's case the damage was significant. (Anonymous parent)

How can we help children overcome the damage of fear and anxiety?

OK, so all of this is pretty bleak and genuinely worrying for people like myself who see first-hand the damage adults have caused to some of our children. However, there is hope, and that hope comes from re-examining the limbic system.

Jaak Panksepp proposed several emotional systems in the mammalian brain. The negative alarm systems of anger, fear and anxiety cause an amygdala response producing stress responses including increased biochemicals such as cortisol. In order to combat these responses, we need to look at the other emotions proposed by Jaak Panksepp. We have already talked about play as an evolutionary survival trait but there are other instinctive behaviours connected to play that also come under the umbrella of pro-social emotions because they promote social behaviour.

Instinctive exploration

What do young children do when they walk past a fence or a wall? They instinctively reach out and stroke the fence. What does a 1-year-old do with a crayon? They instinctively put it in their mouth for a good old taste. What does a child do when they walk through an echoey space? *"Oooooooweeee!".*

Whilst these behaviours are intrinsically linked to play, they fall under another of Jaak Panksepp's emotional systems, CURIOSITY. Now, it might be hard to imagine curiosity as a survival trait, but it is actually the mechanism by which we begin to understand our world, enabling us to survive in it. Like play, it is an instinctive behaviour, influenced by our environment, creating an unconscious, multi-sensory exploration of the child's world. One mistake educators sometimes make is to assume curiosity is a passive system that just requires information thrown at it. The assumption is that children are like sponges absorbing knowledge. The truth is that curiosity is an active system constantly switched on, seeking feedback from the child's world and the people in that world. It uses every sense to find out about the environment and is endlessly sending out questing signals to receive responses. A baby makes noises to illicit a response from the adults in its life; a child bangs a wooden spoon on the wall to gain auditory and physical feedback. Children are not just sponges, they are like sponges with tentacles, continuously seeking responses and actively questing for sensory data.

Earwax tastes foul

Rather unpleasantly, most people reading this will know what earwax tastes like. The reason they know this is because, at some point as a child, their innate curiosity led them to try it. However gross this might be, it is simply a child learning about their world by using their senses. This is common in all mammals. What is not so common in other mammals is the levels to which we take our curiosity. In humans, curiosity breeds ideas, creativity and experimentation, linking that basic limbic system response to our unique upper brain in a way that we don't believe other mammals capable of. The truth is that we didn't just try the earwax once, we repeated the behaviour to re-test our hypothesis that earwax tastes foul. We then move to a whole new level of experimentation when we try to get our younger brother or sister to eat it. This is basic curiosity leading directly to scientific method!

This has huge significance for education. If a learning opportunity activates the curiosity system by being interactive, exciting and multi-sensory then, just like with play, the brain rewards the experience with biochemicals such as benzodiazepines. This creates positive associations with learning, hardwiring into neural networks and making the child want to learn more. If the learning experience is also playful and fun, we are giving children a double whammy of positive biochemicals by activating two fundamental emotions in the limbic system.

The power of curiosity

There is an argument that human curiosity is what has ensured our species dominance over our planet. As predators, we are physically very weak when compared to creatures like tigers or sharks. We cannot outrun our prey and we cannot physically overpower other predators. We are also lacking in super senses. Super senses allow predators and prey an edge when it comes to survival, so a wolf's sense of smell or a falcon's eyesight gives them a significant advantage when hunting prey. Falcons can actually view the ultra-violet spectrum so they can see the urine left by prey such as mice. This must make it a real challenge to be a nervous mouse: *"Oh no, a falcon! Whatever you do, don't wee! Don't wee, don't wee, don't wee! Oops, I've weed. Aaaghhh!"* Humans have none of these super senses or physical abilities. However, our advanced curiosity system has enabled us not just to understand our world but to also bend it to our will. We don't need to outrun our prey when we can build traps, read complex trails and use tools. In short, our curiosity is our super sense, allowing humans to dominate an entire world (for better or for worse!).

The nature of nurture

The third pro-social system proposed by Jaak Panksepp is of fundamental importance to anyone working with children. The NURTURING system is of huge significance to mammals as it is the mechanism for ensuring we protect our vulnerable young into adulthood. Let's be honest, humans need a lot of nurturing. Whilst a kitten is pretty much self-sufficient by 1 year old, a human doesn't seem to be able to fully fend for themselves until much later. Just try leaving your 1-year-old children out in the woods for a few days and you'll see what I mean. (Please don't do this!) I know 30-year-olds who still take bags of washing home to their parents' house!

In order to protect our particularly vulnerable young, we have an extremely potent nurturing system. When an adult makes a child feel safe, emotionally secure and happy, they are nurturing that child and producing a positive biochemical response (including benzodiazepines), making that child feel amazing. They are also producing oxytocin, which not only has anti-depressant properties but also helps to promote social bonding in the first place. Like benzodiazepines, oxytocin is vital for the emotional well-being of our children. The great thing about our nurturing system is that it is a two-way process and when we nurture our children, creating that all-important biochemical response, we also create a biochemical response in ourselves. The tragedy is that there has been a fundamental shift in parenting trends over the last few years. There has been a marked decrease in face-to-face nurturing in some families, along with a corresponding increase in screen time for children. The truth is that a screen is unable to nurture a child to anywhere near the extent of real-life interactions with a caring adult. This means that not only is the child no longer being nurtured but the corresponding nurturing response in parents is also absent. This is breaking a cycle of nurturing and biochemical feedback, potentially impacting on the emotional well-being of the whole family. Remember that, according to Jaak, our nurturing system is an instinctive process based in the limbic system. Just like play deprivation, depriving a child of basic nurturing is the biological equivalent of starvation.

A decline in nurturing?

I recently witnessed a parent outside an inner-city nursery, waiting to be let in. Her daughter in a push chair was tugging at her coat, clearly wanting her attention and repeatedly saying, "Mummy". The mum was resolutely staring at her phone and ignoring the young child. Eventually, after several minutes of this behaviour, the mum turned and shouted, "Stop it, Chantelle, you're doing my f***ing head in!". She then returned to her phone. I am not judging this parent. This was a particularly deprived area and parenting is tough at the best of times, let alone when you are a single parent whose own experiences of being parented are statistically likely to have been negative. The truth is I don't think the parent was aware of the damage she was doing to her daughter. In the UK, parenting training is often very limited. Personally, we had a really good antenatal teacher who taught us how to bathe and feed our baby and change nappies (she also let me have a go on the Gas and Air which was fab!). All of this is useful but at no point did she say, "Play with your child or their brain may not reach its full potential." Or "Turn your phone off and communicate with your child or their speech and language may be impaired!" or even, "Show your child they are loved and nurtured."

OK, so we now have two seemingly opposing emotional systems in the limbic system and, although this may be an overly simplistic way of looking at the brain, it does give us a clear process for supporting children and the most powerful method for ensuring our children's emotional well-being. If we accept that the negative alarm systems progressively exclude the upper brain and diminish conscious thought, it is simple common sense that we need to get the limbic system sorted before any other interventions or developmental progress can be fully effective. Behaviour techniques, for instance, where we explain the child's behaviour to them and expect them to understand the consequences of their actions are rendered pretty pointless if the child is so angry or afraid that the parts of the brain responsible for conscious behaviour regulation are barely operating. We need to get the limbic system right before we can engage the upper brain in any meaningful way.

The good news is that, given time, children can begin to heal the damage caused by anger, fear and anxiety. It is not easy, can take years, and there will be some children who will always bear the emotional scars of that damage. However, I cannot stress enough how much of an impact a positive adult can have on a child. There is always something we can do and the way we begin to heal children is by simply engaging the opposing emotions in the limbic system.

By focusing on Play, Curiosity and Nurturing, we activate the opposing emotions in the limbic system, the natural enemies of anger, fear and anxiety. By simply doing this, we already begin to lessen the impact of the negative emotions. The more children play, in a stimulating environment, where they feel cared for and nurtured, the less they will experience anger, fear and anxiety. Feelings of joy, safety and happiness can begin to replace the negative emotions.

From a biochemical perspective, when children activate the pro-social emotions they produce a cocktail of biochemicals including benzodiazepines, producing substances so powerful that they are prescribed by doctors as an anti-anxiety medication.

Biochemicals of Play, Curiosity and Nurturing

- Oxytocin (anti-depressant, promotes bonding)
- Opioids (similar effect to morphine)
- GABA (anti-depressant)
- Benzodiazepines (brain's natural Valium)

Children also produce BDNF (our oddly named brain growth hormone) which, in addition to growing the brain, is intrinsically linked with brain health and has been suggested as a mediator for vulnerability to stress. In rats, it has also been linked to the damage caused by cortisol to the hippocampus and could potentially mitigate or even prevent that damage. Many anti-depressants increase the expression of BDNF in the brain and there is evidence that anti-depressant drugs protect against or reverse hippocampal atrophy.

In short, through Play, Curiosity and Nurturing, children begin to self-medicate with the exact biochemicals they need to begin to heal the physical damage caused by anger, anxiety and fear.

It is not just the anti-depressant and anti-anxiety properties of Play, Curiosity and Nurturing that make them so potent. There is evidence to suggest that some of the chemicals associated with this area of the brain are anti-acidic in nature, creating not just the "feel good" effects of prescription-grade drugs but also helping balance the acidic nature of stress hormones, creating a bio-chemical balance in the brain and allowing the child to heal.

Margot Sunderland

The amazing Margot Sunderland (a one-time student of Jaak Panksepp) uses these concepts to help children with insecure attachments (2007). If you see her speaking at a conference, she is always worth watching and has massively influenced my practice and my parenting (and this chapter!). She has also written books and produced DVDs.

For me and my organisation, Play, Curiosity and Nurturing have become our fundamental pedagogy because we have seen, time and time again, how life-changing these simple concepts can be. Whatever age of child, whatever vulnerability or social background, it is these three concepts that break down the barriers for our children. Even if the neuroscience and biochemistry leave you unmoved, the profound and transformative nature of these concepts have been witnessed in my long career, too many times for the effects to be merely coincidental. These concepts are utterly life-changing and I firmly believe that if we get these three things right then all other aspects of well-being, development and learning can begin to fall into place. We have to start with the limbic system though and with Play, Curiosity and Nurturing.

Smile, get down to a child's level and let them lead...

My organisation supports Adoption Activity Days by providing play experiences for children and potential adopters. The aim of the events is simple. Some children are passed over for adoption because information on their profile may seem daunting to potential adopters. Behavioural issues, conditions such as autism and ADHD and other disabilities can make it more difficult for a child to find a for-ever family. There are also children who are statistically harder to find families for because they are a little older or have a large number of siblings. Adoption Activity Days are a special party for children where they can play and have fun. At the same time, potential adopters can join in with play and actually meet real children rather than a scary condition on a profile. The events are hugely success-ful at finding forever families for children and we have supported them from the early pilot phase. Before each event takes place, we brief adopters in the best way to interact with potentially anxious children. We instruct them to smile, get down to the child's level and let them lead.

A few years ago, we worked with a young child who was clearly very nervous. She did not speak and was reluctant to join in with our play opportunities. She then noticed something in the corner of the room. She spotted a man with a shiny bald head. Her curiosity system clearly activated and, as she approached this fas-cinating sight, the man smiled at her. Now, as we have discussed, human curiosity leads to creativity and ideas and this young girl had the most amazing idea. She went over to the big box of arts and crafts, took out a bag of multicoloured feath-ers and some glue and began gluing the feathers to the bald man's head. As he had been instructed, he smiled, stayed on her level and let her lead, and soon the most amazing play experience began to take place. They chatted about colours and about the gloopy glue dripping off the man's face, and the child started to smile. I don't know what was more precious - the look of joy on the young child's face, a child who had shown no joy the rest of the session, or the exact same look of joy and wonder mirrored on the bald man's face. Play, Curiosity and Nurturing change children's lives. The curiosity of the shiny bald head, the nurturing smiles and the play that they shared together ultimately led to a forever family.

What does all this look like in practice?

So, what does this look like in practice? Obviously, we need to make our environ-ments as full of Play, Curiosity and Nurturing as possible. We need to find ways to minimise anxiety and recognise that when children are anxious or scared, their behaviour is understandably going to deteriorate. With children who have been through anxiety, we need to be patient, caring and nurturing. This is not always easy. Think of your least likeable child. Yes, you know the one: the one covered in snot whose behaviour has you pulling your hair out. The chances are that other adults in the child's life are equally, if not more, intolerant of this child and consequently behave negatively towards them. You will sometimes find yourself working with children who barely receive a single word of praise in their entire life and for whom the level of nurturing is critically low. And then we expect them to behave? The truth is that our most challenging children are the ones who need us the most, and the best workers find a way to make that child feel special (despite the snot) when potentially every other adult in the child's life treats them negatively. Sometimes it only takes one caring adult to overcome a lifetime of negativity, and we can be that adult if we focus on Play, Curiosity and Nurturing regardless of the child's behaviour.

We also need to recognise that when a child is fully in the throes of their amygdala responses, there is very little point in trying to "manage" their behaviour. One mistake often made is to try to employ behaviour strategies when what the child actually needs is help in a crisis. We can only employ effective behaviour strategies once the child has begun to re-engage their upper brain once more.

Patience and understanding and, above all, helping children feel safe

Last year I worked at a fantastic nursery and afterschool club, delivering behaviour training for parents. However, before the training even started, I observed a clearly distressed parent talking to the manager. He had just come from a "behaviour meeting" at the school about his son who had been struggling in the reception class. The teacher had laid out a behaviour plan for the child which consisted of a series of escalating punishments for different offences. (BTW this is not what a behaviour plan should be.) Whilst listening to the teacher, the parent had glanced at the wall to see the reward chart in the class. Children's pictures were stuck to the chart to represent their behaviour, with a sea of faces on the rainbow at the top of the chart. The boy's father then noticed just one child not on the rainbow but on the rain cloud at the bottom of the chart. Of course, the picture was of his own son. This visual humiliation had deeply upset the parent (not to mention undermining the child). That is not the end of the story though. The brilliant manager of this setting said to the boy's dad that they had had a breakthrough that very evening at the afterschool club. The child in question completely lost his temper, which is understandable considering the day he had probably had at school. Instead of being punished, the child was encouraged into the office where he could rage to himself without hurting another child. All the manager said was that she was "there" for the child if he needed her. Eventually, after a time of shouting the child burst into tears and ran to hug the manager. Finally, his limbic system was under control and he felt safe because one adult was not making him feel worse but was supporting him to cope. (Now that's a behaviour plan!)

Working with school-age children

When working with older children-we need to understand that for some of them the world is a very scary place. Children who suffer from school anxiety feel trapped for long periods of time in an environment that is triggering their amygdala. This is going to impair their ability to learn and potentially affect their behaviour. Once a child is in this spiralling cycle, it can be a real challenge to help them. If every lesson in every school, however, was founded on the guiding principles of Play, Curiosity and Nurturing then not only could school anxiety be eliminated but children's capability, engagement, retention and even, dare I say, attainment, would improve. The limbic system is the foundation of the upper brain and academic learning built on that foundation will be stronger. Remember that when we activate the limbic system through Play, Curiosity and Nurturing, we flood the brain with positive biochemicals. What a wonderful classroom it would be if all of our children, regardless of perceived ability, were literally high on learning.

If every experience in school was based on these three guiding principles, from lesson planning to classroom design, school lunchtimes to parents' evening, then I believe that we would not just have an impact on our children but on our society as a whole.

For afterschool provision, we need to take into account the experiences that a child may have had in their school day and make every effort to help them distance themselves from those experiences rather than merely repeating them. Afterschool provision needs to be special and unique, an oasis of Play, Curiosity and Nurturing in a potentially overwhelming desert of anxiety.

Back to keeping children in at break as a punishment. Don't, just don't! If their amygdala is activated, resulting in impaired learning and negative behaviour, then of course they will not finish their work or behave. The one thing that children in this situation need above all else is respite from their anger and anxiety and a chance to emotionally and biochemically reset. Keeping them in at break will do the complete opposite. It will not improve their behaviour in the long term, it will not make them learn better and is potentially damaging their brain. As the lunchtime supervisor said, "Let those children PLAY!"

But can't fear sometimes makes us perform better?

Now I know what you are thinking. What about those times when nerves have actually improved our performance, when we have overcome our anxiety and exceeded expectations? It is true that within certain tolerances stress can actually improve our performance, sharpen attention and push us to exceed expectations.

However, once we exceed those optimum levels or the stress is maintained for an excessive length of time, we begin to suffer from the toxic nature of those bio-chemicals. The fascinating part is how we learn to tolerate those chemicals in the first place. How do young children "train" themselves to be able to cope with the biochemical responses to anger, fear and anxiety? Through play (you didn't see that one coming! Oh, you did?) The truth is that we train ourselves to cope with stress and danger by playing scary games such as *"What time is it, Mr Wolf?"*, pretending there is a crocodile in the cracks of the pavement or even climbing trees and jumping from increasingly higher levels. More of this vital function in a later chapter.

When play is laden with anxiety…

Another of Perry Else and Gordon Sturrock's (1998) key terms is "dysplay". Dysplay is where the process of play is laden with anxiety and can become less effective or undermined. This is observable in children who have been through stressful situations but can also happen if there are adults present who cause anxiety. Adults can cause anxiety by being overtly threatening such as by shouting, being strict or mean. They can also cause anxiety through towering over children, being unfriendly or simply not making an effort to engage. Children attune their emotions and especially their anxiety levels to the adults in their world, so another way adults can cause anxiety is simply by being anxious themselves. Conversely, calm adults in a child's vicinity can actually lower cortisol levels in the child through a process called social buffering. In much the same way that meerkats have an adult lookout for the playing meerkat children, human children are calmer if the adult they trust is also calm. We all need to be meerkat lookouts for our children to help them feel safe enough to play and avoid dysplay.

Not like other grown-ups?

OK, so what do we do if a child is terrified of all adults? We often work with children who have been through such extreme abuse that they are frightened of all adults. They struggle to form attachments and have had a significant deficit of nurturing in their lives. Once again, the answer is through play. For a child like this, their idea of an adult is not someone who plays but someone who causes fear. Simply by being in the presence of a playful adult, the child can begin to feel more secure. There seems to be a realisation point or stage that the child needs to go through before they can begin to accept us. Obviously, the first stage is that simply by being an adult we are a source of anxiety. The next stage needs to be the realisation, *"She (or he) is not like other grown-ups."* Simply by being playful, silly, dressing up like a banana or being prepared to join in with play, we are showing our children that we may be weird, but we are definitely NOT like other grown-ups. In my career as a manager, it is my team members who have understood this that have had the most impact on children.

I think now more than at any other time in recent history we all need to be "not like other grown-ups". We need to be playful, engaging and nurturing and give our children a respite from the stresses and fears of the world. I truly believe that Play, Curiosity and Nurturing are the difference between children struggling and children thriving.

Playing well with other children?

I often train lunchtime supervisors to support play more at lunchtime and always make sure I work with children at the same time to show that this stuff is not just theory but actually works. One lunchtime supervisor had observed a child exhibiting negative behaviour and decided to physically drag the child to me. She then said in a scathing voice, "you can deal with him". Can you imagine the humiliation and rage this child must have been feeling at being dragged across a playground and then thrust in front of a complete stranger? I took one look at this child and realised there was no way I was going to be able to get through to him in this incandescent state of rage. Remember what we now know about the limbic system. Anger, fear and anxiety progressively erode upper brain function and understanding so no amount of "behaviour strategies" were going to cut it. I did the only thing I could think of which was to instantly get down to the child's level by kneeling. This showed that I wasn't a threat and I further emphasised this by saying, "Don't worry. I'm not going to tell you off. I'm not even a teacher!". I followed this with, "Well, secretly I am a teacher but I teach grown-ups, not children. I'm not going to tell you off or even ask you what happened but I want you to do something for me. It is going to seem silly but I will do it as well. All I want you to do is take a deep breath in and then, after three, I want us both to say our favourite food at the same time. Do you think you can do this?" As you can imagine, the child was expecting to be shouted at and punished and was therefore so completely flummoxed that he actually complied with my odd request, took a deep breath in and then shouted "Pizza". We then had a conversation about pizza and about what are the best toppings (not pineapple, you weirdos). You can probably all see what is happening. Rather than throwing additional fuel on his out-of-control amygdala, I am slowly calming him down. We know from mindfulness that breathing can help us regain control but there is also a little trick going on here. Eating food triggers the limbic system and even thinking about food can produce a small hit of positive biochemicals. So, effectively, I am calming the amygdala whilst subtly activating the positive aspects of the limbic system through positive social interaction (chatting) and thinking about food. Eventually I felt he was calm enough to tell me what had happened. It was the usual story. He was a child with SEND who was consequently "wound" up by other children to the point where he would completely lose it. Once he had told me his tale, he added, "*Are you going to send me to the room?*". It turns out he was sent to a classroom to sit by himself almost every lunchtime because he could not "play well" with other children. I told him there was no need to go to the room and helped him find another group of children to play with and joined in too to make him feel safe. This was the first lunchtime in over a month that he had not been sent to the "room". Whilst in this "calmer" state, I was then able to suggest some strategies to help him overcome his anger and not get into trouble so often.

Reflective Questions

Do your children feel emotionally safe in your setting? It is not enough to simply assume a child feels safe and nurtured. Look at each and every child and make sure there are concrete methods for making sure the child "knows" they are safe and welcome.

Are you and your team doing everything you can to make sure Play, Curiosity and Nurturing are embedded throughout a child's experiences of the setting? Are some of your children arriving at the setting full of anxiety? Examine your welcome and signing-in procedures to make sure a child can overcome their anxiety as quickly as possible.

Are you a different sort of grown-up? Are there ways in which we can shift the emphasis towards Play, Curiosity and Nurturing? Remember that it is not just vulnerable children that need positive limbic system responses.

Chapter Summary

OK, to summarise, play is a key therapeutic discipline, having the most profound effect on the emotional well-being of children. The damage caused by amygdala responses of anger, fear and anxiety is not just emotional damage but also physical structural damage to the brain. Activating the amygdala reduces the capacity of our upper brain, causing an impairment of learning and an increased potential for negative behaviour. The pro-social emotions of Play, Curiosity and Nurturing perform a unique biochemical balancing act in the brain, helping offset the damage caused by anger, fear and anxiety. In order to support children to emotional well-being and positive development, we need to focus first on the limbic system.

I firmly believe that this is the foundation for all successful work with children and have seen so many examples of the most profound change and benefits from simply focusing on Play, Curiosity and Nurturing. We recently purchased wristbands for the team with the words, Play, Curiosity and Nurturing prominently displayed. This is to remind ourselves of these simple concepts. When we are stressed about Ofsted or changes in the EYFS, being harangued by parents or completely undervalued by society, we can glance at our wrists and remember why we are doing this job in the first place.

4

DRAGONS DON'T EAT PEAS – PLAY AS WHAT MAKES US TRULY HUMAN, UNLOCKING IMAGINATION AND CREATIVITY IN A WAY THAT NO OTHER ANIMAL ON THE PLANET IS CAPABLE OF

So far, we have talked about play as a primitive drive shared with all mammals. My observations of my dog Marley have shown that much of the play he enjoys is exactly the same as my own children's play. Just like Marley, my children love running, chasing and play-fighting, they love jumping and balancing and testing their limits and they love being noisy and messy. However, for Marley, whilst this is the most amazing process, it is limited to that primitive survival instinct and for him that is the sum of what play is and always will be.

Children are different. Up to a certain point, they will explore exactly the same play behaviour as all other mammals but then something really special begins to happen. They begin to do something so profound and unique that it defines what it means to be human. They begin to use their imagination. This chapter is all about the weird, wonderful and down-right magical world of imaginary play.

Why is imagination so special?

To understand just how special this type of play is, we need to break down what it means to use our imagination. Think of an object – better yet, put the book down and go and find an object. It may be a pen, a notepad, a banana or even a stick. It doesn't matter what the object is, merely that it has engaged your curiosity for a brief instance (curiosity response in the limbic system!). Every mammal has curiosity and almost every mammal can forage for or chase an object that interests them. Now I want you to do something that no other mammal is capable of: pretend your object is something else. This is not a pen, it is a laser gun; that is not a banana, it is a boomerang for pixies; or this is not a stick, it is a wand. This simple ability to pretend is one of the most profoundly important abilities that humans possess and the very thing that makes us human in the first place.

Now don't get me wrong; we know that some mammals can begin to start on this journey into imagination, but this is nothing compared to humans. Humans have taken this ability to the next level and it is the foundation for almost everything that differentiates us from other mammals. Chimpanzees, for instance, have been shown to have extremely advanced problem-solving skills and demonstrate high levels of intelligence, even to the point of being able to use rudimentary tools. A chimpanzee can use a stick as a tool or a weapon, but no chimpanzee has ever picked up a stick, waved it and said, "Expelliarmus!". The fact is that we don't believe that even our most intelligent animal neighbours have the cognitive or neurological capacity for this seemingly simple process.

Why is this significant? It all boils down to the fact that the ability to pretend things are not what they clearly are is the fundamental basis for symbolic representation. This is in turn the basis for every higher academic function that makes us uniquely human. Complex language relies on the fact that a series of sounds and facial expressions can convey not just simple emotions but also an entire vocabulary of concepts. The word "banana", for instance, does not sound in any way like the noise a banana makes(?). It is a series of noises that bear no relation whatsoever to the curly yellow fruit. Despite this, upon hearing the word "banana" we all instantly identify the noise with the fruit and react accordingly, depending on whether we like bananas or not. This is truly incredible: a simple (and somewhat silly) noise can represent images of a curly yellow fruit, memories of taste, smell and texture, even feelings of anticipation or disgust. Yes, animals can begin to do this. If you shout, "treat" to Marley he will instantly pay attention because the sound has been associated in his brain with him actually eating a treat. Humans take it so much further than this. It is not simple conditioning where a sound or other sensory stimulus creates a response. This is complex thoughts, mental images and concepts creating a sense of "meaning" that transcends anything other animals are believed capable of. In short, our ability for complex communication and language is based on a foundation of being able to pretend things are not what they actually are. Of course, it is not just spoken communication. What are words and letters if not symbolic representations of meaning? The letter "a" looks nothing like the sound it makes (even if that were possible) and yet, from an early age, humans are able to contextually re-arrange those letters to create meaningful written language. Our ability to pass down discoveries to future generations, ensuring technological and societal progress, is dependent on a spoken and written language. This is all based on the fundamental concept of pretending. Think of a number from one to ten. Was it number 7? The number "7" bears no relation to seven objects and yet that symbol conjures up a whole range of concepts and meaning, enabling us to quantify and understand our world. Complex mathematical exploration, language and literacy, artistic expression, storytelling, poetry and numerous other unique processes are all underpinned by the simple ability to pretend things are something they are not. It is no wonder then that Einstein said, *"Imagination is more important than knowledge!"*

This concept is truly mind-blowing. That magical moment when the stick becomes a sword or a wand, when the teddy has a voice of its own or where a child becomes, for one brief moment, a superhero, a teacher or an astronaut, is so incredibly special because it underpins everything it means to be human. When does it first start in human children? The truth is we don't really know. From a very early age, children can identify with puppets and dolls, giving them their own personalities and emotions completely separate from the child. Children can "pretend" to nurture a teddy as if it were a baby, even though it clearly isn't. Regardless of how this process first starts and whatever age of child we work with, these moments are precious and unique and should be supported and encouraged as much as possible. Symbolic play, pretend play, imaginary play, in fact any type of play where the child imagines things as other than what they are, is potentially the most important process not just for our children but for our entire species.

Naked puppet

My son loved his favourite puppet, Lawrence the Lion. Unfortunately, we once forgot to bring him on holiday (the puppet, not our son). Knowing how genuinely upset our son would be, my wife, in desperation, created a new puppet to distract him. The new puppet (named "Nap Nap") was just her hand pretending to talk, a naked puppet if you will. This literal "hand" puppet soon replaced Lawrence as my son's favourite, despite the fact that it looked - well, pretty much just like my wife's hand. Nap Nap had a complete personality and distinct behaviour and my son and Nap Nap developed a genuine friendship which lasted for years. My son was able to project absolute belief and the concept of an entirely separate living entity on to Nap Nap, despite the fact that it was possibly the lowest budget puppet ever. The weird thing is that the power of imagination does not just affect children. My wife once honestly admitted that Nap Nap often said mischievous things that she was not expecting him to say, despite the fact that it was her hand and she was doing the voice for him!

So, the most frivolous seeming types of play are potentially the difference between animals and humans. Imagination is not merely an inconsequential biproduct of our innate intelligence but the mechanism by which our intelligence is able to influence our world and a fundamental building block for our entire civilisation. From our earliest storytelling and cave art to complex feats of modern engineering, imagination has underpinned every single advancement in the history of our species and it all begins with play and with pretending.

Where does imagination sit in the brain?

Those of you who have been following the neuroscience elements of this book will probably now be wondering about where imagination sits in the brain. Once again, this is really difficult to fully assess but there are studies that suggest that imagination is hugely significant and creates massive neural networks throughout the brain. We are no longer looking at the primitive limbic system though, but in the fascinating world of the upper brain. A study that I particularly like is one undertaken by Alex Schlegel of Dartmouth College which demonstrates a

Figure 4.1 Bee with a bull's head drawn by R

huge neural network or "mental workspace" involved in processing imaginary concepts. The amount of the brain activated when adults were asked to imagine simple things in this study was truly staggering, lighting up the brain like a virtual firework display. One of the reasons I like this study is because one of the things people were asked to imagine was "a bumblebee with a bull's head". Doesn't this just sum up the amazing capacity of humanity to be intelligent, creative and silly all at once? I love the thought of using hugely expensive brain imaging technologies, invented by the most creative minds, to explore unique human functions such as imagination, just to find out what happens in our brain when we think of a "bumblebee with a bull's head".

Let us just think for a second about the importance of this and other similar studies. If imagination creates a huge neural network in the upper brain and induces a "firework display" of brain activity, even when thinking about the silliest things, then it must logically have a huge potential for brain growth. Remember that brain growth is experiential and parts of the brain that are used grow whilst areas not used simply don't. However, in imagination we have potentially one of the most powerful tools for physical brain growth simply because it activates so much of the brain. In addition, the neural networks of imagination overlap with many other processes such as communication and language, mathematical thinking and problem solving, making it a profoundly important and neurologically rich process.

An imaginary life?

My daughter has an alarmingly vivid imagination. She did not have an imaginary friend but created an entire imaginary life with imaginary family, multiple imaginary pets and an imaginary house. We would have conversations with her nursery key workers where the key worker would say things like, *"Oh, I hear you have a new horse? That sounds lovely".* Obviously, we don't have a horse, but my daughter was so unerringly consistent and convincing in her make-believe that you would sometimes find yourself believing her world more than the real world!

Imaginary sit-ups?

Another thing I found interesting about this and other studies was the fact that imaginary experiences affect the brain in the same way as real experiences. When imagining the bumblebee, for instance, activity was noted in the Occipital lobes where we process images from our eyes. This is odd as the people taking part in the test would most likely have had their eyes closed during the scan. With all sensory input to this part of the brain effectively removed, why then did it still show so much activity? Simply because the test subjects were imagining an image which activated the part of the brain associated with processing images, despite it not even being a "real" image. If you imagine throwing a ball, for instance, the parts of your brain responsible for processing how you physically throw, controlling your limbs, aiming, etc. will also activate even though you are not actually throwing the ball. Now I know what you are thinking: Can you build a six pack by imagining sit-ups? I have tried and sadly it doesn't work. However, you can theoretically improve your ability in a sport to some extent by imagining taking part in that sport. This is sometimes used by sports psychologists to help athletes retain their abilities when injured, by imagining the perfect jump, serve, goal, etc. even when they are physically unable. It is not just sport though; imagining playing a piano will boost neuronal connections in regions related to the fingers. The potential for this is enormous and I find it utterly fascinating, especially when we look at the impact on children. It also has huge implications for our environments. We may be limited by our physical environment, but we should never be limited by our imagination. Even in the most dull and unstimulating physical spaces, we can create imaginary experiences that affect the brain in the same way as "real" ones.

Imaginary play clearly has a huge capacity for supporting brain growth and potentially underpins an incredibly broad range of developmental and academic processes. In the UK, however, it does not seem to be given the priority it needs, with academic subjects often taking precedence. In UK primary schools, there are attainment tests called SATS which focus on Maths and English. Not that I agree with these tests in the first place, but where are the tests for imagination? Where are the tests for Art, Drama, Music or storytelling? In addition, I often hear from our parent groups that imaginary and pretend play is something that parents find particularly challenging and it can make them feel embarrassed. We also know that statistically parents are now less likely to read bedtime stories to their children than previous generations, which is a crucial opportunity for developing imagination (and also empathy, creativity, literacy and speech!). With the huge increase in screen time and decreased opportunities for imaginative play, we are potentially critically undermining children's developmental potential.

Divergent thinking

One reason this is not just crucial for our children but for our society as a whole is to do with how we solve problems. The ability to solve problems creatively and come up with innovative solutions is a vital component in the advancement of our species. There are many names for this type of thinking – divergent thinking, lateral thinking, even "thinking outside the box" – but the underlying premise is the capacity to creatively solve problems. The term divergent thinking was first coined by psychologist J.P. Guilford in 1956 and was used to describe ways of thinking that create multiple solutions to a problem. The opposite of this is "convergent" thinking where we follow a logical series of steps to solve a problem or achieve a specific outcome. Now don't get me wrong, there is nothing bad about convergent thinking. We all need to pass exams or put up certain Swedish flat-pack furniture from time to time and convergent thinking is a valid and often essential process for this. The problem is that life is not convergent. Life will throw us curve-balls where logical steps won't help. There will often be a piece missing from the flat-pack furniture or the instructions are solely printed in Swedish. There will be times when all of the obvious solutions simply won't work. This is when we need to be divergent thinkers. We need to innovate and creatively problem solve, coming up with multiple solutions to our complex problems and using our imagination.

When you look at people who have changed our world, you will see that they tend to have something in common. The most influential scientists, architects, entrepreneurs, doctors, artists, mathematicians and musicians (to name just a few) are all divergent thinkers. They share the ability to think creatively and innovate. Why then does our current education system focus so heavily on convergent thinking?

House, monkey, plane...

One way to look at divergent thinking is the different ways in which we approach building Lego. In the olden days, we would have a huge box of assorted Lego and would build (without instructions) whatever our imaginations led us to create. A house, a plane, a monkey? A house that turns into a monkey plane? This is divergent thinking in a nutshell: looking at a large box of random bricks and seeing multiple solutions. However, some modern children will now only build the model that is on the front of the box by following the instructions in a series of steps. The pieces themselves have become more specific and less generalised. The model then stays on the shelf. This is the essence of convergent thinking.

So how do children become divergent thinkers?

Once again, what has this to do with play? Well, it is all related to how we become divergent thinkers in the first place. Psychologist J. Nina Lieberman (2014) proposed that the traits associated with divergent thinking in adults are intrinsically linked to playfulness in childhood. Interestingly, Lieberman defined playfulness as three differing types of spontaneity. The potential for children to be physically, socially and cognitively spontaneous is linked to the ability to creatively problem solve. Children need to have the spontaneity to be able to move things from one place to another and add them to other things to create something new. They then need the social spontaneity to discuss and negotiate freely within their environments and the cognitive spontaneity to solve problems their way without always being told what to do. This spontaneity within the environment is a vital developmental criterion and potentially lacking in some children's experience of childhood.

Lieberman also cited overtones of joy and sense of humour as aspects of playfulness. I cannot overstate how important joy is to the emotional well-being of our children and could probably write a whole book on this vital and completely undervalued concept (idea for a sequel?). It is also really refreshing to see sense of humour cited as an important developmental process rather than something to be crushed in our children! What Leiberman was basically saying was that if children experience a spontaneous and joyful childhood (filled with playfulness and humour), they are more likely to exhibit the traits of divergent thinking in later life.

Playfulness

- Physical spontaneity
- Social spontaneity

- Cognitive spontaneity

- Overtones of joy

- Sense of humour

This fits in perfectly with my own observations of children. The potential of children to be spontaneous equates to working with their brain, fulfilling those limbic system urges to play and be curious, flooding the brain with biochemicals. This in turn creates a firework display of imagination in the upper brain where children are using their creativity to solve problems of ever-increasing complexity.

Loose parts play – working with the brain!

This brings us nicely onto loose parts play. The original theory, proposed by Simon Nicholson in 1971, simply states that in any environment, 'the degree of inventiveness and creativity, and the possibility of discovery, are directly proportional to the number and kind of variables in it'. In short, any resource or environment that offers multiple possibilities (or variables) has intrinsically greater play value and contributes more to the development of creativity and imagination. There are similar methodologies such as heuristic play and open-ended resources, and in all of them the main aim is to allow children to freely experiment and innovate within their environment. This is accomplished by creating possibilities or variables within an environment by using resources which lend themselves to creative uses. Rather than single-use specific toys, loose parts play will involve items such as cardboard boxes, pipes, scraps of material and other random objects that can be combined to create something greater than the individual components. This increases the potential for spontaneity within the environment and increases the number of variables or possibilities. When children begin to see multiple possibilities, they are beginning to think divergently.

Two pieces of string...

My father grew up in London just after the Second World War. His family was always short of money and he had very few toys to play with. Occasionally, the newspaper seller would give him the piece of string that the papers were tied in - or, if he was lucky, two pieces. With two pieces, he explained, 'I could be a twin-engine plane!' My father saw not just string but the possibilities of the string, including aeroplane propellers. He went on to become a successful aeroengineer, working on engines for Concorde amongst his achievements and an innovative and creative thinker all of his life.

In short, the brain structure, mindset and imagination my father needed to be a highly innovative aeroengineer was developed through play with the simplest of resources.

Developmentally, this is massive for children. Loose parts play creates a virtual neurological gateway between those wonderful limbic system urges and the firework display in the upper brain, enabling children to interact with their environment in exponentially more creative and imaginative ways.

Compound flexibility

This is the cornerstone of a theory by Dr Frasier Brown (2003) which extends the theory of loose parts play. In his theory of compound flexibility, he equates those possibilities or variables to the degree of flexibility in any environment. He describes two potential cycles: one in which there is limited flexibility in a child's world and another in which there is a higher level of flexibility (or variables). In the limited environment, there is a decline in interactivity, experimentation and positive responses and consequently there is a stagnation in the relationship between the child and their environment. The fascinating part of this theory, however, is something I have observed countless times in the best settings. In a highly flexible environment with increased opportunities for experimentation and control, the range of positive responses (including biochemical) is much greater. Children are able to increasingly innovate and be spontaneous within those environments and this creates a cycle of ever-increasing interactivity and creativity. This in turn leads to children now being more able to innovate in less enriched environments and to be able to look at the dull and unstimulating and to use their imagination to create something magical.

Stoney Drainy anyone?

OK, this is one for the older readers (you know who you are). If you had roller skates that were metal, adjustable and fit over your shoes then you are the people who will remember this. You would have been stood around on a street corner and you would have been bored. Then you may have noticed a big stone and a drain cover and spontaneously invented the game of "Stoney Drainy" which you would have played for hours before making up a new game. The dull environment you found yourself in was no barrier to play as you were able to see possibilities even in a non-flexible environment. Why could you do this when sometimes modern children struggle? Because when you were bought a present at Christmas you would play with the box instead. Because you grew up when Lego was making random creations from a big box of bricks and when playing out was the norm. Most importantly, because you had a clothes horse that you could make dens with. RIP the Clothes Horse.

So, throughout this chapter we have seen those fascinating links between the basic limbic system urges of Play and Curiosity and the firework display or neural activity in the brain caused by imagination, between the biochemical responses of spontaneous loose parts play and divergent thinking and the ever-increasing potential of compound flexibility. I think veteran early years specialist Sally Thomas said it best though: "I don't do activities with children. I give them experiences."

Remember that brain growth is experiential so not only are we supporting children's imagination, creativity and divergent thinking, we are also growing their brains.

Curiosity as a pedagogy

The Curiosity Approach focuses on this wonderful link between the primal curiosity system and those wonderful explorations of stimulating resources. Created by Lyndsey Hellyn and Stephanie Bennett, the focus is on providing stimulating environments full of curiosity and joy. Having seen some of Stephanie Bennett's nursery settings first-hand, I can honestly say that the impact of this freedom of exploration and curiosity on children is massive.

The future workforce

The World Economic Forum published its Skills Outlook for 2022 (World Economic Forum, 2022). They list "declining" skills and "growing" skills needed for the jobs of the future. Basically, they are detailing which skills are going to be more important for the future workforce and which skills are going to be less important. This gives governments and education establishments insight into which areas of education to invest in to give our young people the most effective skill set for future employment. Shockingly, on the list of declining skills are reading, writing and maths – the only things we test children on in the UK. On the list of "growing" skills, we see creativity, originality and initiative, complex problem solving and critical thinking. We also see emotional intelligence. Loose parts play and imaginary play are not just ways of making children have a better childhood, they are preparing children for the future.

What does this look like in practice?

In any environment working with children, we should be providing opportunities for children to imagine and create without fear of failure. We need to provide opportunities for children to freely explore their environment and live in the moment. Remember that exploring increased the production of BDNF, the brain growth hormone, in rats. Crucially, we should be modelling imagination and creativity by our behaviour and innate sense of the magical. We should be telling vibrant stories and encouraging children to play pretending games. It is very easy to assume that imagination play and storytelling are just for early years settings but every child of every age can benefit from imaginative experiences. I have been doing interactive storytelling for many years and it has been just as effective with our 14-year-olds as with our 3-year-olds.

The key component of any environment for children is not resources, but the human and emotional environment provided by positive staff. The same is true of loose parts play; it is as much about human interactions as physical resources. If the practitioners are encouraging, supporting and modelling possibilities, then the children will begin to do the same.

If a practitioner can show joy in their environment, expressing awe and wonder in the remarkable connections children make through loose parts play, then children can begin to explore the myriad possibilities inherent in their environment. If the practitioner is uninterested, nervous, or limits exploration and experimentation, then the child's relationship with the environment can stagnate.

How does a child know that a box is not just a box until they see a practitioner randomly wearing one on their head? How does a child know that there can be possibilities in their world if they are not encouraged at every stage to experiment and investigate their environment in their own way? How can they become divergent thinkers and see multiple possibilities if every 'activity' has only one goal or possibility? If activities are continuously outcome driven, then we limit the possibilities open to a child. Loose parts play should always be an experience, rather than an activity, and is as much a mindset and ethos as it is a selection of resources.

The bottom line is that children, not adults, decide which resources are 'loose parts' and adults need to model, support and nurture a child to see beyond the literal and into a world of possibilities.

Supporting the joy of discovery

One thing I like to do is take a big box of interesting rocks and stones to a setting and scatter them around the outside area before the children arrive. Some are out in the open and some are hidden. I don't tell the children they are there or give them any instructions, I just wait until children are playing outdoors and watch the simple joy of discovery as they find them.

Humans are capable of the most incredible feats of imagination and children are able to maintain a powerful suspension of disbelief to the point where the imaginary world is often more powerful than the real one. A part of their consciousness must be aware of the pretend nature of the play and yet they maintain consistency of imagination throughout. This is wonderful to observe but also incredibly powerful developmentally.

Another example of this utter belief in the imaginary world is that like most families with dogs we have a pretend voice for Marley so that we can reply on his behalf. *"Did you just eat that cushion, Marley?"* to which my wife or I will reply in Marley's voice, *"No, Daddy, it must have been one of the cats!"* Now I come to write this, it does sound a bit weird and maybe this is just us? My daughter was lying about having played with the dog when clearly she hadn't. I said in Marley's voice, *"She hasn't played with me at all, Daddy"*. In genuine anger, my daughter turned on Marley and shouted, *"Stop lying, I did play with you!"* Despite being 9 years old and completely aware on one level that it was me talking, the incredible power of imagination caused a genuinely angry response directed not at the true source of the irritation but at the imaginary source. This uniquely human ability to completely believe in the imaginary has probably led to some of our greatest achievements and also some of our worst atrocities. Only time will tell which of them my daughter will accomplish (although I'm leaning towards the latter!).

I am fortunate to work in many different settings but two of them are unique in that the buildings are almost identical to each other. However, they have a completely different ethos when it comes to their outdoor space. Both reception classes have a tarmac outdoor area. In one school, the outdoor area is almost entirely made up of loose parts play resources. There are crates, boxes, leaves, sticks, material and pipes as well as access to water, soil and inevitably mud. The other has bikes, scooters and several plastic climbing frames and play houses. Now don't get me wrong, children love scooters and bikes and there should always be opportunities for children to experience these. However, if you observe both settings for only a short time, you will see the most incredible difference between the same-age children at each site. The children in the loose parts environment are a constant whirlwind of activity as they build, destroy, transport and stack. They create complex structures to transport water from the tap to the mud pit. They solve problems such as a bucket with a hole in it and how to carry larger bits of resources with the help of their friends. The adults often do not interact with the children for long periods of time but are always available to help with additional resources or even to join in if asked. The whole experience is a joy to watch, let alone be a child who is part of the process. The other setting is just ordinary. It is not bad practice; children are engaged with the various resources and staff are having lovely interactions with the children. It is only when you compare the two settings that you see the fundamental difference in the children themselves. The independence, confidence and problem-solving ability of the children from the loose parts environment is significantly and visibly advanced when compared with the children from the other setting.

The other thing about loose parts play is that it is fundamentally more in line with how children are meant to learn. Let's be honest, we all know that sitting still and listening to a grown-up speak is the least effective form of learning. Freely exploring, experimenting and actively learning are far more powerful in terms of learning as well as being considerably more rich neurologically. There are some children who, regardless of intelligence, do not respond well to formal education. Children often struggle (I know I did) with the sitting still part, let alone the listening part of formal learning. Exploration of loose parts resources is anything but passive. I often visit primary schools and deliver loose parts sessions with children. I will dump a load of resources, such as cardboard boxes and material, in the hall or outside in the playground. I will then stand back and let children freely explore the resources. Almost every time someone will say, *"Aren't you going to tell them what to do?"*. Within ten minutes, the same teachers will be saying things like, *"I've never seen Leroy so engaged before!"* or *"Jessica is normally so quiet".*

The zipline of doom

I once worked with a group of older children with quite severe behavioural issues. One boy, James, was 11 years old and had been excluded from several schools for his behaviour. His social worker told me he had recently been called "stupid" by a teacher and just did not get on with education at all. He had been passed from foster carer to foster carer and was clearly struggling. We took the young people out into the woods and gave them access to a whole range of loose parts play resources such as ropes, nets, material, etc. These could be combined with the loose parts resources found inherently in a wood such as trees, branches and sticks. James asked me if he was allowed to make a zipline. I said "of course", and gave him some ropes and asked him to come and get me if he needed anything else. Now I will just mention that making a working zipline has been a long-term ambition of mine. Unfortunately, the ropes I buy are too "elastic" to make a good zipline and every one of my attempts (and hundreds of children's) have ended in failure. It is still fun to try though and so I happily let James give it a go. I nearly had a heart attack twenty minutes later when I noticed he had not only managed to tension the ropes perfectly, he had created a really steep angle and was about to launch himself down his fully operational zipline. I did not want to undermine such a brilliant achievement, so I simply offered to stand at the bottom and catch him, to prevent him hitting the fence if he went too fast. I will never forget his reply:

"There's no need, mate. I've put a brake on it."

Not only had he engineered a perfectly effective zipline, he had thought to fit a working brake on it, using an additional rope that would prevent anyone reaching the fence and injuring themselves. There is only one word for someone like that: "Genius!". This was a child who had failed at every school he had ever attended and even been called "stupid". We all tried the zipline, had the best afternoon ever, and everyone agreed, James was a legend.

The wonderful world of Immersive Narratives

OK, back to imagination. One really nice way to create magical imaginary experiences with children is the Immersive Narrative. Immersive Narratives is a phrase I coined several years ago to describe the make-believe scenarios that we regularly created for our children. I was asked to speak at an international conference about the process and so I needed to give it a posh name; hence Immersive Narratives. All it really means is that we would set up an imaginary situation in which children and staff all join in the make-believe together and then we saw where the situation took us. It is probably easier to explain it with an example. One of the earliest I remember was when we told the children that a spaceship had crashed in the grounds of the children's centre. NASA had been in touch and asked if we could help collect any bits of spaceship and also to be on the look-out for alien life. We all proceeded outside where we had scattered old foil containers and anything silver we could find in our store across the entire playground. Children ran around collecting shiny things with a feeling of excitement far beyond what would have been seen if we had just asked them to collect shiny things. Meanwhile, one of our staff was gradually transforming into an alien. She began with green rubber gloves and then slowly added bits to her costume, leaving the alien mask until last. Children obviously noticed this and asked, *"Why are your hands green?"* to which she would reply, *"Hmm, I'm not sure but let's get on with finding those spaceship bits".* In order to conjure up a mental picture, please don't assume the costume was in any way realistic (or even very good). It was clearly obvious exactly who the member of staff was, even once the mask was donned. However, the minute the final piece of costume was in place the atmosphere in the setting transformed. Children began pointing at the staff member and saying in hushed tones, *"Ben, it's an alien!".* There then followed a whole series of interactions between an alien (who did not speak English) and a group of children who acted in every way as if this was a genuine first-contact moment, despite it clearly just being Deirdre in a rubbish costume. Eventually, the alien managed to communicate that it was frightened and wanted to go home, so the children helped the alien build a rocket out of cardboard boxes. The alien stepped into the rocket and waved goodbye. At this point, it was snack time so reluctantly the children went in for their snacks. When they rushed back outside, the rocket was gone, Deirdre was herself again, and all that was left on the playground was a note that said, *"Thank you for helping me to find a way home, from Snarsguggle".* The children talked about this "real" event for weeks afterwards.

Now you may be thinking that this is a lovely thing to do with your under 5s but we also did the same Immersive Narrative with our 5- to 10-year-old group with exactly the same results. I mentioned in a previous chapter the young man I met who had valued the project so much. Whilst reminiscing with him, he said, *"Do you remember when that spaceship crashed?"* He didn't say, *"Do you remember when we **pretended** the spaceship had crashed?"* He would have been about 7 or 8 at the time.

Immersive Narratives can be really simple or quite complex and the only rule is that all the adults join in with the make-believe. It is not as effective if one member of staff is looking on with arms folded, saying, *"What are you silly lot up to?"* A nice simple one is just to tell the children someone special is arriving. The children decorate the room or prepare gifts or whatever is appropriate for the moment when The Queen of the Fairies, a Pirate or even the real Queen walks through the door. Yes, they all know it is you in a costume, but they maintain the make-believe because it is a moment of true magic and excitement. Just remember, when you are feeling foolish dressed as a pirate or the queen, what you are doing for the children's brains.

There's a leopard in the garden!

You don't have to be confident and outgoing to join in make-believe. I know it can seem daunting at first, but I promise the benefits to children make it worth giving it a go. One of my students on the Play Champion course admitted she was not confident enough to do an Immersive Narrative with her children. Rather than pushing her too far out of her comfort zone, I suggested she do some cardboard box play with her children instead. However, the following week she ran up to me and said *"I did one!".* She had brought a leopard-skin print onesie to work and a cheap leopard mask and then whilst the children were inside, she had crawled around the garden area. One of her co-workers then ran to the window and shouted, *"Children! Come quick! I think there is a leopard in the garden".* The children were spellbound but one of them noticed that the leopard was limping and holding its paw up. The children approached the leopard with genuine trepidation (even though they knew it was not a real leopard) but with real determination to help bandage its injured paw. They then spent several minutes petting the leopard and treating its injured paw. My student had been absolutely terrified of the idea of dressing up and pretending but had to acknowledge that her children had experienced something truly magical that day and her manager admitted it was one of the best days she had ever witnessed at the nursery. She was already planning her next Immersive Narrative and one of her fellow key workers, who just happened to own a tutu, was arriving the following week as a fairy princess.

Supporting, not undermining

As adults, we can lose track of the imaginary and it is easy to forget how compelling imagination is to children. It is easy to belittle or undermine imagination play as silly or even pointless. Many adults do not believe they are imaginative themselves and therefore find it difficult to support imagination and creativity in children. The truth is that all adults and children are creative as it is a fundamental element of what makes us human in the first place.

Figure 4.2   Giant cardboard dinosaur – in fetching yellow and blue

The problem is that, in many cases, our own experiences of childhood have falsely made us believe that we are not creative. Often, our education takes a very narrow view of creativity, restricting it to a few media or disciplines. I was repeatedly told as a teenager that I was no good at art simply because the majority of lessons involved us trying to copy something dictated, not by my own curiosity, but by the teacher. I have never been very neat, cannot do fine detail and get easily bored by unstimulating tasks (sound like any children you know?). I consequently grew into adulthood believing I was not in any way artistic. It took working with children to build a giant T-rex out of cardboard boxes to make me realise we were all just as creative as any artist. When you look at a bright yellow and green 12ft-tall T-rex, nobody is being critical if it is not very "neat" or if the painting is not expertly shaded. All anyone can say to that is "Wow!"

Once again, Sally Thomas said it best. Only the tiniest proportion of art is on paper and the smallest part of that is copying something someone else has done. Art is every way in which a child expresses themselves creatively. Every time a child jumps over the paint pots in joy, they are being just as creative as if they used them on paper.

Adventures in time and space

One of the most creative Immersive Narratives I ever witnessed was in a nursery setting where they built a time machine out of cardboard. Half of the children got inside whilst the other half put on fake beards they had made out of cotton wool. When the time travellers exited the machine, all of their peers had aged 50 years and had white beards. Obviously, some of the children had not a clue what was going on as time travel is a complex concept even for adults. They simply enjoyed the fun of going on an adventure and dressing up. Some children, however, were saying things like, *"I'm like my grandad!"*. Also interesting was the fact that all of the female staff put on fake beards too as if that is what they believe they will look like in the future?

We just need to immerse ourselves in the children's world of imagination to see how powerful this can be and maybe rekindle some of our own creativity. The best bit of advice I can ever give to settings and individuals who wish to promote more imagination and creativity is quite simply to acknowledge that nothing is ever impossible. If you work in a bank or an office, you can't put everything on hold and suggest that you travel to the moon instead of working. Working with children, however, you can do this on a daily basis. Make a simple rocket out of cardboard and spacesuits out of old bits of material and you can travel anywhere in the universe. So long as you remember to walk in slow motion due to the low gravity when you exit the spaceship, it doesn't matter that you are still in the afterschool club or nursery or your back garden. This may sound silly but genuinely, if you have a whole staff team enabling children to see possibilities by embracing the seemingly impossible, you are creating the foundations for divergent thinking, not just in your children but in your adult staff too.

Nothing is impossible

In our afterschool club, we once had our funding for swimming trips cut. One of the staff was going to tell the children that sadly the trips were cancelled but I suggested we should do the swimming trip on site despite not having a pool. The next week, the children brought their swimming costumes and basically pretended to swim across the outdoor games area whilst staff threw buckets of water at them. This was more memorable than any actual swimming trip and the children absolutely loved it. The simple belief that nothing is impossible enabled us not just to save children from the disheartening experience of missing out on their swimming trip but also to create something new and magical for them which was talked about for months.

When I first started my company working with children, the strapline for our play team was "Putting the magic back into children's lives". I subsequently had to change this as people kept mistaking us for magicians which as you can imagine made me really cross. (Don't get me started again on magicians!) However, I still stand by this as a really important thing that we as adults can help our children to experience. I do believe that childhood is very different now than it was for my generation and I believe that opportunities for imagination have declined. I think it is really important that we acknowledge this deficit and do everything we can to bring a little magic back into our children's lives and, who knows, we may just be creating the dreamers and creators of the future.

Reflective Questions

Think about your environment. Would you consider it to be enriched? Does it have a high level of interactivity and lots of variables? Are children encouraged to see possibilities? Do children have access to resources with multiple uses and are they supported to combine resources? Are children given enough time to simply explore and experiment?

Are there opportunities for pretend play? Do the adults in the child's world join in pretend play? Are our stories for children vibrant and interactive or dull and static?

Try an Immersive Narrative. Start with something simple if you don't feel confident. A nice one is to sit in rows and pretend you are on a train or plane and then when you "arrive" you pretend you are somewhere else: the Moon, the bottom of the sea, the future, a fairy kingdom, Skegness, etc.

Are your children having a magical childhood or an ordinary one?

Chapter Summary

So, to summarise, our ability to "pretend" is not merely frivolous but an underpinning factor in almost every aspect of higher learning, from mathematics to literacy. Children learn to pretend through imaginary play, through stories and through projecting their own imaginary space onto the real world. The use of simple imagination creates a firework display of activity in the brain which makes it potentially a huge factor in brain growth and development. Divergent thinking or the ability to think creatively is a contributing factor in human civilisation and is developed in childhood through play and playfulness. The use of non-prescriptive resources such as loose parts play can unlock this wonderful process.

One of my cousins (not a real cousin but a friend of family-type cousin) loved to pretend she was a dragon. By that I mean she behaved like a dragon at all times and actually seemed to believe she really was a dragon. I will never forget when her exasperated parents were trying to get her to eat her dinner, she shouted with utter conviction, "DRAGONS DON'T EAT PEAS!". To be honest, we all thought she seemed a bit strange. She is now a successful writer. Maybe she was a little strange but clearly her imagination has been crucial to her success in adult life and this must be connected to the imaginary play she experienced in childhood. Or maybe she really was a dragon all along!

5

CROCODILES, DANGER AND CERTAIN DEATH (WELL, MILD BUMPS AND BRUISES) – THE INESTIMABLE IMPORTANCE OF RISKY CHALLENGING PLAY

OK, so where does my problem with magicians start? Many years ago, we hired a magician to attend one of our projects. He wandered around doing magic tricks for children and finished with a fantastic magic show. Unbeknown to us he was secretly appalled at the dangerous things we were allowing children to do and subsequently complained to the Health and Safety Executive. When I say dangerous things, I am of course referring to the mud slide, climbing trees and leap-frog. All things that we took for granted in our setting. We then had a complaint-driven inspection of our setting where we had to defend our practices to the Health and Safety Officer. Luckily, the Health and Safety Officer agreed with our assessment of these activities and also agreed that they were an important part of our work. The only thing that he wanted removed was, very bizarrely, the stinging nettles from our nature area. I argued passionately about the stinging nettles being an important aspect of nature in an inner-city area. Eventually, the Health and Safety Officer allowed us to keep our stinging nettles which was a victory I felt really proud of. The very next day, I fell head-first into the nettles and my whole face swelled up for about three days. Was it merely a coincidence that soon after the magician visited our setting, my face was painfully swollen, or was the magician to blame all along?

What really struck me (apart from the nettles) was how different the magician's view on safety and risk was to our own. Why did he see things as dangerous that we thought of as ordinary childhood experiences? So, this chapter is all about the controversial subject of risk and challenge and what we can do to help our children experience this vital process.

When I was a child, our school caretaker would throw a bucket of water down on a freezing cold day to make an ice slide for the children. Admittedly, this was over 40 years ago but the difference between then and now in terms of attitudes towards health and safety is staggering. Now a bucket of sand or grit is the only thing the caretaker or premises officer is likely to throw over an icy playground. Obviously, children's safety has to be a priority and the last thing we want is for our children to be injured. However, has excessive health and safety come at a price?

The simple answer is yes. The fact is that risky play teaches children to deal with dangerous situations in later life. Risky play develops our physical capabilities to cope with actual danger by conditioning our responses and body movements to minimise injury. When we climb, jump and inevitably fall, we train our bodies and brains to protect us when we are most vulnerable. The mistake many people make is assuming that children are more vulnerable than adults when it comes to physical injury when in fact the opposite is true. First, children are closer to the ground simply by virtue of being shorter. This means they can fall over more safely than adults. Children are also a lighter weight, meaning that impacts with the ground have less ... well, impact. Finally, children have bendier bones. Children have a much higher ratio of cartilage to bone which means their bones break less easily than adults' do. What this boils down to is that childhood is the ideal time to take risks, that is when we are less likely to sustain serious injury. Children's injuries also heal quicker!

One for the accident book...

Whilst working on the inner-city project, we had a child fall off a tree and bang their knee quite badly. Upon examining the injury, we saw that the child's knee had become massively swollen and misshapen to the point where we became convinced we needed to call an ambulance. The child did not seem to be in much distress, but the knee was alarmingly swollen and distended. We were about to call the ambulance when one of our team suggested we roll up the child's trouser leg and check his other knee. The other knee was equally swollen and misshapen and it turns out this child just had exceptionally knobbly knees. No ambulance was required and he was running around again five minutes later!

What is risky play?

Sometimes even the name "risky play" can put people off. I have heard it called adventurous play, exciting play and we sometimes even call it exhilarating play. The play theorist Bob Hughes (2002) describes risky play as one of his 16 play types in his taxonomy of play types. However, he refers to this type of play as "Deep Play", so you will sometimes see it called that, especially if you work in a Playwork environment.

The best definition of this kind of play came when, for a play strategy consultation, I interviewed a group of children in Rochdale about all aspects of play and in particular about risky challenging play. One very astute girl really summed it up for me when asked to describe what risky play meant to her. She looked at me as if it were the most obvious thing in the world and said, *"it's just stuff that makes us excited and makes our heart beat faster"*.

I think this is a really useful definition as it actually looks at the feelings and effects of risky play, rather than trying to identify what specific activities constitute risky play. As we will discuss later in this chapter, what is risky for one child may not be risky for another, but the feelings and physiological effects will be the same. So, whatever you want to call this type of play, we are discussing those wonderful moments of childhood that push us outside our comfort zone and make us excited and make our heart beat faster.

One thing you will notice when working with children is that they will often actively seek risk: pushing themselves to climb that little bit higher or jump down just one more step. This instinctive desire to push themselves suggests that, just like Jaak Panksepp's other play behaviours, risky play has a significant survival potential. It actually makes sense if you think about it. Preparing for real-life danger by "playing" will make the child better able to survive falls and other dangerous situations by giving them the physical and emotional tools to cope when they are adults. Play is, after all, children's training to be adults and adult life is not always "safe". This innate urge to test their limits is a key factor in physical and even emotional resilience.

I would even go as far as to argue that risky challenging play has a potential to improve life expectancy. Simple common sense would suggest that being able to fall better, assess danger better and minimise injury must have an impact on a person's ability to survive.

Carefully controlled cartwheels?

I encountered a school recently where they had banned cartwheels at lunchtimes. I wrote an impassioned email to the head teacher, explaining how vital a simple cartwheel was for the physical and cognitive development of our children. She replied that the children could still do cartwheels but only in a carefully controlled gymnastics lesson. I think this is quite sad. Cartwheels and similar expressions of joyful movement existed long before "gymnastics" and are so intrinsically important to our development that the risk of minor injury becomes insignificant. Can children injure themselves doing cartwheels? Of course they can. Does this mean that no child should experience that joy of movement except in "carefully" controlled lessons? Cartwheels, handstands and a whole range of challenging movements and "stunts" are part of that instinctive drive to create the strongest version of ourselves we can be. Most importantly though, they give a unique joy that would be impossible to replace in a structured lesson and may be the closest thing to flying children will ever do.

Another interesting thing to consider is that our immediate, instinctive responses to danger need to be appropriate to the specific dangerous situation. If we have instinctive responses to "fight, flight or freeze" then each of these responses increases our chance of survival only in an appropriate situation. But what if we get the wrong response? When I was a university student, I was running at full speed through the corridors (yes, still running in corridors even as a young adult) and surprised a friend of mine who was walking the other way. He was so startled by my appearance (I have that effect on people) that he simply froze in place and I cannoned into him, knocking us both sprawling. His instinctive reaction of "freeze" was clearly the wrong response in this case (obviously not my fault at all!). How do we know the correct response? Well, if other aspects of survival are developed through play then it makes sense that this ability is also linked to the risky challenging experiences we have as children. This can be critical though. If a child is in a dangerous situation, for instance being in the road when a car is approaching, it is vital that they reflexively access their "flight" response which would be to quickly move out of the way of the oncoming vehicle. Defaulting to a "freeze" response in this circumstance could be life-threatening. Training our brains and bodies to cope with fear and respond accordingly is a critical aspect of development and life expectancy and I believe the best way to engage this process is through risky challenging play.

Practising to survive

When I was young, I had a scooter which I would race around on for hours. I soon learned that if you hit a kerb at speed, you would be flung over the handlebars to land in a painful heap. Undeterred, myself and a few friends spent an entire summer practising this action until we could fly through the air, clear the kerb entirely and land on my front lawn, roll and then come to our feet triumphantly like scrawny, scabby gymnasts (the scabs were from all the times we had failed before finally perfecting this difficult stunt). Why is this significant? Last year I bought my daughter a scooter. This scooter had a fundamental design flaw which only became apparent when I was hurtling down a hill at some speed. (Obviously I had to test it out for my daughter – I wasn't playing, honest.) The front wheel locked and I went straight over the handlebars. Instead of landing with an almighty splat, I flew through the air, rolled and landed on my feet. A couple of teenagers on the street gave me a grudging round of applause. Now I should stress that I am not a gymnast, I am neither fit nor agile and am in my 50s. What allowed me to survive a genuinely harrowing and potentially dangerous accident? The simple fact that I spent a whole summer practising that very manoeuvre over 40 years ago.

Bumps and bruises…

Now the controversial bit. I believe it isn't just the risky challenging play that is beneficial. What about the injuries themselves? I am convinced that the bumps and bruises we experience in childhood also have a vital role to play in the development of resilience. There is no way to passively teach children how to cope with pain. It is something that needs to be experienced first-hand to help develop appropriate responses. I am not suggesting for one second that we deliberately injure children or even put in place opportunities for pain, but we do need to acknowledge that children *will* fall over and hurt themselves and that this is the very mechanism helping to develop their responses to danger and pain in later life. The problem comes when we repeatedly restrict children from even the simplest of explorations of this vital process. Whilst our priority must always be to protect our children from injury, I think as a society we have gone too far. I am not talking about children experiencing serious injuries and I don't think we are even discussing genuine risk here, merely the simple things that we all took for granted when we were children. Climbing, jumping or balancing, where the risk is a bump or a bruise, should be a natural part of childhood and I believe it is hugely significant for our children's well-being when we prevent these experiences. It is worth noting that on the latest safeguarding training I attended, "over-protecting children" was cited as an example of emotional abuse:

> Emotional abuse may involve: Imposing expectations that are inappropriate to the age or development of the child - e.g. over-protecting the child, limiting their exploration and learning, preventing them from taking part in normal social interaction.

So, where has it all gone wrong? Why are children no longer experiencing anywhere near as much of this type of play as previous generations? I believe the culture of litigation that exists in the UK has forced a level of health and safety stringency on us that has become potentially stifling for the development of our children. There was a time in the not-too-distant past when you could buy "sanitised" soil for use in nursery settings and every corner had to be rounded and every surface flat and slip free. The good news is that this is no longer always the case. The ceaseless adverts for *"no-win no fee"* injury claims - *"Have you been injured in a trip or fall that wasn't your fault?"* - have steadily declined and the Health and Safety Executive in the UK has made clear statements that over-protecting children damages their development and that we need to balance risk with positive outcomes for children. Things are definitely improving but realistically we are never going to get back to the days of caretaker-constructed ice slides for children!

Risk-benefit analysis

This brings us nicely onto the fascinating world of risk assessment! Seriously, although risk assessment may seem dull, it is a unique opportunity to be realistic about what will actually happen rather than always leaping to a worst-case scenario conclusion. In addition, the Health and Safety Executive is now recommending a risk-benefit analysis approach to risk assessment. This means that rather than the old risk assessment, which only focused on risk and probability of risk, we now also need to consider the benefits to children and factor this in when making our judgement. A classic example is climbing trees. It would be easy to simply ban all tree climbing as dangerous, but every single tree is different. A risk-benefit analysis looks at the realistic risk of your specific trees but then also looks at the benefits to your specific children. This allows us to make a much more informed decision on whether to allow climbing.

It often helps when working out the benefits to group them, so I always look at:

- Physical benefits
- Emotional benefits
- Cognitive benefits

For climbing a tree, this is an easy task. Physical benefits may include balance, strength, coordination and flexibility. Emotional benefits would be things like sense of achievement, confidence, self-esteem, access to natural materials and the natural world. Cognitive benefits might include problem solving, brain development, developing risk management strategies and overcoming challenges. You then make the judgement based on the two factors. If you believe that the risk to the child outweighs the potential benefits, you do not allow tree climbing (but do try to find alternatives!). If, however, you believe the benefits outweigh the minor risk of injury, you allow tree climbing, carefully supervised if necessary, and watch the joy on your children's faces.[1]

Now don't get me started on the "cold compress". Years ago, we had first aid kits with bandages and plasters, antiseptic and even safety pins (or 'tiny silver death-bringers' as they subsequently became known). Gradually, these items were removed from the box as new rules due to allergies and other health issues were introduced. Eventually, we were facing an almost empty box scenario, with almost nothing we were allowed to "treat" children with. At that point, some bright spark came up with the cold compress.

The mysterious origins of the cold compress?

I always imagine a meeting somewhere with very important people discussing what to do about the empty first aid box issue and the fact that people would complain if we didn't at least do something for children's bumps. After hours of deliberation, someone piped up, *"We could always wet a bit of toilet paper and treat the injuries with that?"* *"Hah"*, replied another important person, *"People would never fall for that as a treatment … unless of course we give it a posh sounding name. How about … the cold compress?"*

---

[1] Forest School training offers really useful guidance on tree climbing, height, safety, etc. This can be invaluable for raising the confidence levels of staff.

Fast forward a few years and in some settings there are queues of children with insignificant injuries lining up for the obligatory cold compress. I am not saying that the comfort value of a cold compress is without worth. There is evidence that on some injuries, sprains for instance, cooling the injury can help lessen recovery time[2] and we know that cooling a head bump reduces swelling. However, children already recover from injury much faster than adults, bruise less and experience less pain. Of course, legally, we need to treat and record head injuries, and in fact any non-minor injury, but there is really no need for a cold compress on a slightly bruised knee or elbow. The medical benefits are minor, but the eroding of children's physical resilience could be significant if they have to run to an adult to get a cold compress every time they hurt themselves the tiniest bit. I know this is controversial and please don't be offended if you don't agree, but it can make a huge difference to a group of children if we move away from over-treating insignificant injuries. We are advising lunchtime staff in schools, for instance, to acknowledge the minor injury and then suggest the child carries on playing for five minutes and come back if it is still causing them pain. Nine times out of ten, the child gets caught up in playing again and forgets about their bump or bruise. And remember that whilst children are playing, they are producing benzodiazepines which are actually prescribed for painful injuries such as back damage. We will still treat more serious wounds and always treat and record head injuries as this is a legal requirement, but I believe everyday bumps or bruises are best treated by playing, just as most of us did when we were children.

The problem with this approach is not the children. They soon learn that playing through the pain is effective and they stop coming to a staff member as often when they are injured. In short, they develop physical resilience and their own coping mechanisms for pain. The issue is that some parents complain if their child does not receive obvious treatment for an injury, however minor. This is not in any way blaming parents because we all want to protect our children from harm and want to know they are being well looked after. We always send a letter home to parents before we introduce this approach, explaining exactly why children may get bumps and bruises and why this is actually OK. I have included this letter as an appendix in case anyone feels it would be useful.

The emotional and biochemical context for risky play

Getting back to risky and challenging play, this type of play is not just about physical development and survival. The emotional impact of achieving and

---

[2] But even this is up for debate.

pushing oneself to new limits is also crucial for children. Possibly the most important developmental process, though, is teaching children to cope with the feelings that we experience when we encounter dangerous or stressful situations in later life.

By playing with fear in an emotionally safe context, children train their bodies and brains to cope with the feelings and indeed biochemicals associated with fear. This can impact not just on a child's ability to cope with danger but the ability to cope with life itself and can have a significant impact on confidence and emotional well-being. Because of this, children need to jump off sofas, climb trees and roll down hills. They need to pretend there is a crocodile in the cracks in the pavement and scream and laugh when the wolf chases them in *"What time is it, Mr Wolf?".*

For many years I struggled with this paradox. I know that fear and anxiety are intrinsically bad for children, yet I also know first-hand that experiencing fear through risky challenging play is an incredibly powerful development process. I struggled to understand how both of these facts could be true at the same time. Of course, now we know about the biochemistry of play it all makes sense. Yes, fear is bad for us because it activates our amygdala, flooding our brain with potentially toxic biochemicals. However, when we experience fear in the emotionally secure context of play, we are offsetting the dangerous chemicals with the positive biochemicals associated with play. This means that we can practise activating our amygdala in an emotionally and biochemically secure context, allowing us to cope better with these emotions in later life. This kind of suggests that one of the most developmentally rich sounds you will hear from a child is the "laugh-scream". Combining fear and joy, this unique sound is a sign that our children are experiencing a broad limbic system response, enabling them to "train" their brains to cope. So, the next time you play "What time is it, Mr Wolf?", why not make the wolf extra scary. (Please don't traumatise your children though! Make sure they are still laughing and not sobbing.)

So, risky challenging play is essential for children but one size most definitely does not fit all. What we are looking for is balancing the stressful feelings and hormones of danger with the positive feelings and biochemicals of play. This is going to be different for different children in the same way it is for adults. Some of you reading this may have done parachute jumps or bungee jumps, showing you have a very high "risk threshold". Other people reading this might steal a biro from a training course, just for the adrenaline rush. The trick is not to throw all of our children off a roof because "risk is good for you". The trick is to find out what gives each child that wonderful balance of fear and excitement. Some children will find excitement going a little faster on their tricycles whilst others may need to jump from alarming heights and push their bodies (and the sanity of the adults around them) to the limits.

Pushing the limits

I once worked with a 15-year-old boy who could jump off a 5-metre climbing frame, roll on the grass and get up with no injury whatsoever (I kid you not). I was criticised by another member of staff who could not believe I would allow a young person in my care to do such a dangerous activity. I had been working with Ahmed since he was 4 years old. I explained to the other worker that Ahmed had jumped off the first rung of that climbing frame when he was 5 years old. When he was 7, he could jump off 3 rungs and 10 years after that first tentative jump, could successfully jump off the top of the climbing frame which no other child could achieve. What right did I have to stop a young person fulfilling a goal 10 years in the making? The child had demonstrated at every stage a fundamental understanding of risk and employed coherent risk management strategies throughout, ultimately leading to something quite amazing. (It was still terrifying to watch!)

Because of children's broad range of responses to different risk levels, it is not always helpful to think of it in terms of "activities" but once again think in terms of "experiences". What we are really looking for is for each child to push themselves a little and experience something that gives them that unique mix of fear and excitement. Risky challenging play therefore becomes much more about "feelings" than about how high a child should be able to jump at a particular age or stage. I also think that if we look at risky challenging play in this light, it becomes less scary for us to implement and gives us more scope to support each individual child. If we focus on the feelings created by risky challenging play, it also gives us much more opportunity to offer alternative approaches when we inevitably have to stop an activity because it is actually dangerous. Rather than stopping the activity cold, we can offer an alternative that engenders the same feelings in the child: *"Thea, come down from those railings and come and do some colouring"* is not going to cut it but, *"Thea, come down from those railings, let's jump off the climbing frame instead",* just might. If we understand that the feelings engendered by risky play are vital to development, we can more easily find alternative approaches to support the individual child.

Imaginary experiences

It is also worth remembering that imaginary experiences affect the brain in the same way as real experiences. This opens up a whole range of alternatives and indeed a whole sub-branch of imaginary play. In "What time is it, Mr Wolf?" we know the wolf is not real and we know that it won't really eat us, but we still scream when it is "DINNER TIME!". The crocodile in the cracks in the pavement is not real but still gets a squeal of fright when we accidentally step on a crack. You can even expand on these imaginary experiences by creating Immersive Narratives. We are going to cross the river on this tight rope which might be a real rope but could just as easily be a chalk line across the floor, but with the right imaginary atmosphere (wind noises from the children?) a real sense of jeopardy can happen.

I am definitely not saying that we can replace all of the lovely challenging experiences a child physically needs with imaginary play. They do still need to climb and jump and test themselves physically, but it is definitely worth bearing in mind that these wonderful imaginary experiences can support some of the same level of emotional development as real activities and, as an added bonus, light up the brain like a firework display at the same time.

What does this look like in practice?

So, what does this look like in practice? The issue at the moment is not that health and safety observance is stopping children doing things that are dangerous but that it is stopping children doing things that are statistically not dangerous. Whether we are parents, nursery staff, school or afterschool settings, this means that we need to simply re-examine what our children are and are not allowed to do. There may be a very good reason why an area is "out of bounds" or a particular experience is not feasible, but we need to be sure that it really is a good reason. By looking at the area or experience and realistically assessing risk and then factoring in the benefits to the child, we can be a lot more transparent and clear about what actually constitutes risk.

The other issue, of course, is the huge variance in adult risk thresholds which means there is often an inconsistent approach to risk. Some members of staff and even parents will allow the child to do things that another may not (and the child will quickly work out who to ask in each case!). This is because the issue of what is realistically dangerous and what only appears dangerous is very rarely discussed in the staffroom or even between parents. So, the first step to help our children experience positive risky challenging play is that we need to actively have that discussion. We need to be discussing what are the children allowed/not allowed to do and why, so that every member of staff is singing, if not from the same hymn sheet, at least in the same church.

Jumping off the sofa!

One of the things I do on my parent play sessions is to ask them to draw a quick sketch of something they used to play when they were children. This is a great way to uncover those lovely play memories and start a discussion about how valuable those experiences were. One dad at a nursery setting drew the following picture:

Figure 5.1   Jumping off a shed roof onto a tree swing!

This is a picture of the dad, aged 7, jumping off a shed roof onto a rope swing. This looks truly terrifying but led to a really useful discussion about why it is so important that children experience risk. The dad left the session feeling very thoughtful as he had freely admitted, like most of us, that he over-protected his daughter and was constantly telling her to "slow down, be careful, get down from there, be careful, don't jump so high, be careful, etc.".

Three weeks later, Emily (the man's daughter) proudly announced at nursery, *"I'm allowed to jump off the sofa now!"*. The amazing thing is that in that three weeks the nursery staff had noticed a startling change in Emily. She seemed more confident, was engaging in things more enthusiastically and was even communicating more. Only three weeks after the dad had started to support play rather than restrict it, there was already a noticeable difference in Emily's development. The dad wasn't allowing anything actually dangerous, he wasn't throwing her out of a window or wrestling with bears (at least I hope not), he was simply allowing Emily to be a child again and push herself and her limits on her terms.

Steering rather than restricting

The other thing we need to be doing is steering rather than restricting. We need to find viable alternatives to the things that we, sometimes for good reason, don't allow our children to do. We need to come up with interesting and imaginative solutions when our environment does not lend itself to risky play and help our children experience this vital developmental process.

One thing that can help both parents and settings is to have a flexible approach to risk and challenge which can adapt to meet changes in the environment and our children's individual abilities as they grow. The risk-benefit analysis can be really helpful with this as it allows us to make in-the-moment judgements about risk as it happens, rather than shutting down children's play without thinking. Taking that moment to think, "what could realistically happen?" and then, "what are the benefits to my child?" allows us to make informed decisions based on conscious thought, rather than a snap decision based on fear. These "in the moment" assessments are called "dynamic risk assessment" as they are flexible to meet the changing circumstances.

A slippery slope

I was once supervising an activity for older children where they were racing down a hill on old bikes with no brakes (don't ask!). At this point, Shina, a girl who used a wheelchair, asked me if she could race down the hill in her wheelchair. Even at the time, with very little experience of working with children with disabilities, I did not feel I had the right to stop her when everyone else was having so much fun. Assessing the situation, I determined that the hill was not very steep and she was fully in control of her wheelchair so I allowed her to take part. She consequently raced down the hill and had the time of her life. Now, unfortunately, I did get into some trouble over this. Not only did some staff members think I had gone too far but Shina's parents also came to the setting to complain. However, their complaint was not at all what I was expecting. They actually thanked me for making Shina feel so included and part of the group and they had no problem at all with her racing down the hill in her wheelchair. What they did have a problem with was me, as an adult, having a go in the wheelchair afterwards as it was a £2000 custom-built wheelchair and not a toy! The truth is that Shina had had so much fun, she then invited the rest of the group to have a go in the wheelchair too, which of course we couldn't refuse.

Whether you believe I was right or wrong for letting Shina race down the hill, the truth is that I was even then conscious that every child deserves the same rights to a vibrant and exciting childhood. I have since worked with numerous children with disabilities and frequently deliver training on inclusion and disability, and nothing has changed that viewpoint. Interestingly, when the document "Managing Risk in Play Provision" was published, which was a Play England commissioned document endorsed by ROSPA and the HSE, they were unambiguous that all children are currently being restricted from opportunities for positive risky play. However, the document also made it very clear that children with disabilities are even more likely to be over-protected and have just as much right to these kinds of play experiences as any other child. So, I believe I was right to let Shina race down the hill but definitely not right to then have a go in her wheelchair.

Reflective Questions

Examine your current practice and realistically assess whether children are able to test their limits and experience risky play. Look at individual children. Can a child experience excitement at our setting at whatever level they need? Are there ways in which we can increase levels of risk and challenge but still be happy that children are protected from serious harm? Think about the team you work with. Is there a consistent approach to risk and challenge or are children getting mixed messages?

The wind in his face...

Fast forward to my current role and I was working with a group of children with a wide range of disabilities. Ethan, another wheelchair user, had to wear an oxygen mask for a majority of his day and could only remove it for short periods such as when he was eating. Whilst doing a superhero-themed game, one of my team decided, with his permission, to remove his mask for a short time and replace it with a superhero mask just like everyone else was wearing. She then pushed him around the playground at great speed whilst he pretended to be flying. As had happened so many years before, I again received a complaint from a parent, this time for removing the mask for something as frivolous as being a superhero. In this case though, I was incredibly fortunate to have taken a photo of the child. (I wish I could show you!) If you ever wanted a definition of the word "joy", it was the look on this child's face as he zoomed around the playground feeling the wind on his face for potentially the first time in his life. The parent took one look at the photo and instantly agreed that it had been the right thing to do. Ethan was in no real danger but was experiencing the wonderful excitement of moving fast and the simple joy of being a superhero. Was it risky play? Well, he was definitely excited and I guarantee that his heart was beating faster, so, yes, for that child at that time, this was risky play that was profoundly important and truly magical.

Figure 5.2   Superhero in a wheelchair by K

6

GET THAT OFF YOUR HEAD: YOU'LL MESS YOUR HAIR UP! – THE CATASTROPHIC EFFECTS OF PLAY DEPRIVATION

OK, let's get bleak for a second. I know it is probably stating the obvious but if we accept that play is hugely significant for children's well-being and development then it stands to reason that a lack of play is detrimental to children. In this chapter, we are looking at play deprivation. We are discussing the terrifying neurological cost of the decline in play and the current crisis in children's mental health.

I still remember the long days of the summer holidays that seemed to go on forever: traipsing about with my friends from morning till evening with no adults in sight; digging holes, climbing trees, finding a dead frog and then chasing my friends around with the dead frog on a stick. These experiences may not have always taught us what we know but, more than anything, they made us who we are. These experiences are largely absent from some children's lives now.

Play deprivation is a loose term for a series of symptoms caused by a lack of play. Not every child has every symptom and, of course, not every child is play deprived. However, there has been a significant decrease in play over the last 50 years, with potentially huge implications for children. I genuinely believe that even my own children are play deprived when compared with my experiences of childhood.

First though, I just want to briefly talk about screen time. I don't want to come across as someone who hates all screens and thinks we should all go back to a pre-electricity era. In fact, I love screens. I love watching films and TV, can't get enough of my iPad and phone and even play console games from time to time. To be honest, I could not do my job without screens and my whole life would be worse without technology. I don't want to completely stop children having access to these wonderful inventions. However, I do worry that, for some children, technology has replaced something extremely precious about childhood.

Do we know for sure that screens are actually bad for children? There is all sorts of contradictory research on the benefits or detriments of screen time for children. Some say that over three hours is potentially damaging to the brain, whilst others say that screen time speeds up visual reaction and processing of sensory input. Some studies suggest that screens for under 2s are extremely damaging and there is a whole range of studies around the negative effects of the blue light inherent in close-up screens such as iPads. There are also studies that show the educational benefits of these technologies. If you are interested, just do a Google search on the subject and you will see hundreds of articles and studies. You don't need to do this though. Just observe a child watching a screen and compare that with a child digging a hole. Just look at their eyes and you will have your answer right there. The hollow, blank look of a child passively accessing a screen is a world away from the vibrant, excited (sometimes mischievous) look in a child's eyes when they are play-ing. I don't advocate removing screens from children entirely, but I do believe that every hour a child spends on a screen is an hour they are not climbing trees or making mud pies, using their imagination or being physically active. I do believe that excessive screen time is genuinely bad for our children, but I also believe in balance. I think these technologies can bring a lot of benefits to our children, but this should never be at the expense of play. The average screen time in the UK is now seven hours a day for children. That does not leave too much time left for the important business of playing.

It should also be noted that in one of the studies on screen time that showed deterioration in the brain after three hours of watching television, it was also recognised that content and context were important. A family watching *Strictly Come Dancing* together, booing and cheering the judges, etc., are engaged in a high degree of social interaction, whereas a child sit-ting alone with their tablet is going to have a markedly different experience and a much higher potential for negative effects.

OK, so regardless of your views of screen time, if we examine the benefits of play it stands to reason that children need as much of it as possible. Whilst there are playful uses of screens such as games and apps, they will give only a fraction of the benefits of "real life" play. It is also going to vary massively from child to child. So, what general symptoms would we expect to see in children that have not played enough? In no particular order...

Negative behaviour

I could write an entire book on behaviour (there's an idea?) but to keep it brief, lack of play has a direct impact on children's behaviour. If you think about what play does to the brain it is pretty obvious why. Play offsets negative emotions such as fear, anger and anxiety, all of which are pre-cursors for neg-ative behaviour. From a biochemical perspective, play creates that wonderful biochemical mix, the optimum chemicals for emotional well-being. These are sometimes called pro-social emotions in that they actually support positive behaviour. Quite simply, children who feel good behave better. I have often worked on sessions with children with "challenging" behaviour only to find that they have forgotten to misbehave because they were having so much fun. Not only that, but by reducing anger, fear and anxiety, children are more able to engage their upper, more self-aware brain. Empathy, moral code and ethics all reside in our upper brain. In short, our ability to know right from wrong is impaired by anger, fear and anxiety, and so by reducing these emotions through play we allow children to make informed decisions about their own behaviour choices.

Aggression

Directly linked to behaviour is aggression. Without an outlet for the primal drives associated with play, children can be come easily frustrated and this can quickly turn into aggression. Also remember that play is a key way of off-setting anger which is intrinsically linked to aggression. When we become angry or scared, we become more aggressive because our amygdala is preparing us to fight a threat. Some studies have suggested that, in extreme cases, lack of play can lead to severe anti-social behaviour and violence.

I once worked in a young offender institute, teaching young fathers how to nurture and play with their children when they finally got to see them on the outside. This was a heart-breaking project for many reasons, but during one session there was a prison-wide lockdown which meant I was stuck in a room with these young men for several hours. I taught them how to make paper aeroplanes as one of the only resources we were allowed to bring into the prison was paper. There are only so many things I could teach them how to make out of paper so eventually we ended up talking about their childhoods. Not one of those young men could remember a single moment of play with their parents.

Physical delay

We have already mentioned the fantastic Sally Goddard Blythe and her research on neuromotor immaturity. The truth is that things are getting steadily worse. More and more children are less physically able than they should be due to lack of simple movements in childhood. Where do children experience a majority of these movements? Through play. The increase in screen time is leading to a significant decline in physical activity, with potentially catastrophic results for our children.

Communication and language delay

Once again, this is a subject for a whole book. Children primarily develop language through playful interactions with adults: nursery rhymes, singing games, stories, peekaboo and making silly noises. Responsiveness is key and the playful "conversations" between a child and a parent, for instance, have a profound effect on the child's vocabulary and language development. That is the important part to remember. A television can introduce a variety of words to a child but that simply isn't enough. Without the back-and-forth conversations and responses from another person, language development becomes significantly less effective. Once again, it is the playful interactions that often seem so frivolous that profoundly impact on a child's development. In addition to this, we have already discussed the huge overlap between neural networks in the brain and a lack of simple physical play will not just impact on physical development.

Anxiety and mental health issues

Mental health is a genuine crisis in adults as well as children, with ever-increasing numbers of people experiencing some form of mental health problem in their lifetime. The bottom line is that play helps. When working with children who have been through trauma and who have clear anxiety, it is those little moments of play that seem to make all the difference. We have already discussed play as one of the most powerful therapeutic disciplines a child will ever experience, and without it we are only increasing the potential for negative emotions and mental health issues. It is no coincidence that the decline in mental health in children has matched a corresponding decline in play.

We often make magic potions with children (no, we are NOT magicians). It is a simple idea which many of you will have tried before. Children add food colouring and sparkly confetti to a bottle of water and then shake it to make a potion. The clever bit is that we put an old torch in a box so when you put the potion on top of the box it lights up and sparkles. When we do this for our most vulnerable children, there is a moment of the purest awe and wonder. Even though the children know it is simply a torch in a box, the potion for that brief moment becomes truly magical. The simple delight in this tiny moment of play has the most profound effect on the mood of the children and it has so often been a turning point in our children becoming more emotionally secure with us. These simple moments of play massively impact on children, reminding them that though the world can be a dark and frightening place through play there is still some magic. Maybe we are magicians after all!

Poor social skills

None of the aspects of play deprivation discussed in this chapter have been at all surprising and in fact, if common sense prevailed in our society, we could alleviate many of these symptoms. This one is no exception. Play is a key way in which children learn social behaviour and so without it children may struggle.

Figure 6.1   A "magic" potion! There is a torch hidden inside this cardboard box which makes the potion look really magical!

You are probably all thinking of children you know now? We don't learn how to navigate our social world through screens but, once again, through those playful interactions and social games that happen with real people. This is something you can observe first-hand in children. I visit many nurseries and schools and it is wonderful to see staff members modelling positive social interaction, appearing interested in their children (even when they want to talk about dinosaurs for the 100th time!) and having genuine conversations even with very young children. These playful conversations are so vital for language acquisition but are also a uniquely powerful process for children in them becoming socially aware and growing as social human beings.

My son was put on "the Rain Cloud" for talking when the teacher was talking. The rain cloud is part of a potentially damaging system for reward and consequence used in some UK schools. He was, at age 5, baffled by this: *"But the teacher was talking when I was talking?"* he said.

Now I know that children sometimes need to listen in class and that they need to understand that when someone talks it is polite to keep quiet and listen to them. However, it seems odd that developmentally we are so desperate in early years for our children to move more and talk more and yet they are suddenly told to sit still and be quiet. Social skills require advanced brain development in the upper brain and these things can't be taught. Children require two-way conversations to develop social skills by interacting with other people in their world. What we can do is model social behaviours and support our children to engage in play experiences that encourage social behaviour. It is also worth bearing in mind that sitting still is a fine motor skill that requires a significant amount of brain/body control. You need to do big movements to develop small ones, so you need to move and play freely to develop the ability to sit still.

Poor spatial awareness

Once again, common sense dictates that if you excessively access your world through two dimensions you will have more difficulties when navigating three. This is one of the reasons screens for under 2s are considered particularly risky. Young children are constantly developing their ability to recognise and navigate their world. They do this through all five senses and even two additional senses to work out where they are in relationship to their world. Vestibular is our movement and balance sense which tells us where our head and body are in relation to space and gravity. Proprioception is the sense that allows us to know where our body parts are in relation to each other. Try touching your nose with your finger with your eyes closed – you should be pretty close. Proprioception also gives us feedback in terms of knowing how much force to use to accomplish tasks such as picking up an egg without cracking it or accidentally pushing another child over. How do we develop all of these incredibly complex aspects of navigating the three-dimensional world? Don't worry, play has got it covered! Being able to navigate the physical world can increase survival potential so children will instinctively do things to develop this ability. Children will instinctively spin around (as discussed in Chapter 1). If they see a hill, they will roll down it; if they see a wall, they will balance on it. At every age and stage of development, children will instinctively do whatever is most developmentally appropriate to build this vital survival skill so that, as adults, they can navigate a huge variety of environments and surfaces. Not one single aspect of those vital abilities comes from watching screens.

Interestingly, the need to "spin" around to develop our balance is only really needed in childhood and so the urge to do this will decline as we get older, and once we reach around 25 years old we no longer seek out this behaviour. This is probably because we have already developed it as much as possible and so the biochemical reward is no longer present. This is borne out by the fact that once we get to a certain age most of us no longer enjoy roundabouts. In fact, many parents reading this will have made the mistake of taking their children on the "Waltzers" or similar fairground ride because they remember how much fun it was as children. If you are over 25 (as an average), you will have soon discovered how horrible these rides are when you are no longer producing benzodiazepines to offset the unpleasantness and nausea!

The roundabout of doom!

I remember taking a group of young people on the "Centrifuge" which was a horrible ride from the olden days which has now probably been banned by the Geneva Convention. I used to love roundabouts and was really enthusiastic about persuading these 13-year-olds to go on the ride with me. At 27 years old, after the first minute of the ride I felt so ill I was scared I was going to die. After the second minute, I felt so ill I was scared I *wasn't* going to die. I no longer needed this experience to develop my balance.

Play is more important than this though. Play also helps us build up our world picture, our sensory context and our place and even size within it. It may sound strange but knowing instinctively roughly how big a door is, or how far away the horizon is, for instance, allows us to instantly assess all other objects in our environment and build up a mental picture of scale. This is essential for navigating our environment and we only build up this "world picture" from real-life interactions with the world. One of the reasons children constantly try to climb onto things is not just to improve their physical ability but also to access the world from a slightly altered perspective (higher up) so that they can accurately map their environment. This is hugely significant for spatial awareness to such an extent that astronauts landing on the moon found it very difficult to calculate the actual size of objects because the distance to the horizon was different to that of earth. Once again, you simply cannot gain this ability by watching screens.

Poor risk management strategies

As we discussed in the previous chapter, play teaches children to deal with dangerous situations in later life. By playing with fear in an emotionally safe context, they train their bodies and brains to cope with the feelings and indeed biochemicals associated with fear. This can impact not just on a child's ability to cope with danger but to cope with life itself and can have a significant impact on confidence and emotional well-being. Because of this, children need to jump off sofas, climb trees and roll down hills. They need to pretend there is a crocodile in the cracks in the pavement and scream and laugh when the wolf chases them in *"What time is it, Mr Wolf?"*. Play is the only way a child can experience fear in an emotionally secure context, so if these experiences are completely absent from a child's life they may struggle with both mental and physical resilience.

Decline in physical activity

We have already discussed how catastrophic this is for children. The problem is that the more a child disengages in physical movement, the harder it is to re-engage them and a passive lifestyle becomes the child's preferred mode. This can have disastrous long-term health implications and is a key factor in obesity. Working with children is as much about challenging entrenched cycles of behaviour as helping them develop. We all know how much fun it would be to run around jumping in puddles or make a bow and arrows out of wood and string. The trouble is that these things take extra effort. We know our children will benefit but they first have to get coats and wellies on and then they may need an adult to supervise so we also have to put our coat and wellies on. In the end, it is far easier to let the experience come to us via a TV or tablet. Sadly, these experiences are not only passive in themselves, providing only a fraction of the benefits of physical activity, but they also further entrench the passive behaviour until it becomes all the child ever knows. Because of this, play deprivation does not just mean that a child does not do enough physical activity but that they also won't want to do enough because they are caught in the cycle of passive activity. The only way we can combat this is through joy. If we can rekindle a joy of physical movement through play, we can make the extra effort worthwhile so that the screen time becomes a poor substitute for actually playing. This means, as parents and even childcare workers, we have to break our own cycles of inactivity and inspire joy in our children through our own playful and joyful explorations of movement (this can be really difficult but is so worth it). Put on some music and dance with a big grin on your face, like you just don't care, and see how much movement your children do when they join in.

The healing power of play

One of the things I am most passionate about is sharing the message of play with parents. I put on special play workshops to help increase play in the home as much as possible. I originally thought of the idea because we were running "Stay and Play" sessions with a Children's Centre and I noticed that parents were not playing with their children at all and were standing around chatting. In fact, one of my staff nicknamed the sessions "stay and swear" because every so often a parent would stop chatting to shout swear words at their children when they misbehaved. The first session was not at all popular. The parents had been repeatedly badgered to be there (with real badgers) and were very reluctant, if not directly hostile towards me. One lady in particular was very negative and sat at the back with her arms folded. In fairness, she did attend the training on crutches so some of her mood may have been due to the fact she was in pain. However, the change in the group when I finally persuaded them to play was staggering. The turning point came when we made dens and the grumpy lady stole the biscuits to secretly eat in her den. She started grinning and joining in with all of the subsequent play experiences. At the end of the session, we had a fashion show with costumes made from old bits of material (to show that play does not need fancy resources!). This lady put two sports cones down her top and flounced down the "catwalk" dressed as Madonna. Ten minutes after the session finished, there was a knock at the door and the previously grumpy lady walked into the room and said, *"Sorry mi duck, I've forgotten my crutches."* She picked up her crutches and left. Now I know what you are thinking: *"Did Ben heal that lady? Was it a miracle?"* I believe that she became so caught up in the positive feelings of play that she forgot for a moment that she was in pain. And remember, benzodiazepines are prescribed for pain relief!

Myopia

Now most of this list has been common sense and probably something you could have spotted in your own children. This one is just bizarre though. Not many people know that we are currently in the midst of a myopia epidemic. Myopia is another word for short-sightedness and currently there are more children who are short-sighted than at any other time in recent history! The reasons for this seem obvious. Anyone with an iota of common sense would guess that increasing screen time has got to be an issue. The problem is that the evidence on this is hard to come by as close-up screens such as tablets and phones are so relatively new an invention that there are few long-term studies. I strongly suspect that we shall shortly see those studies directly linking phone and tablet use to poor eyesight. That aside, one factor we know to be significant is that outdoor play has massively decreased when compared to previous generations of children. Why is this important? The eyes contain muscles and, just like every other muscle, they need to be built and "trained" during childhood. You train your eye muscles by simply focusing on a range of different distances. Indoors, we can focus on the short distance and maybe the middle distance. It is only when children are engaging in outdoor play that their eyes constantly focus on all distances, from the very close (look at that ladybird) to the far distance of the horizon.

This constant seamless movement from short to long distance focusing, that only occurs during outdoor play, is how we train our eyes for the rest of our life. Consequently, because these experiences are now absent from children's lives they are significantly more at risk of becoming short-sighted. I don't know about you, but I find it heart-breaking that our continuing disregard for the importance of play and our ever-increasing reliance on screen-based technologies is taking away the eyesight of our children.

Bone health and more

The decline in outdoor play is not just damaging children's eyesight and their physical activity levels. There are numerous studies linking outdoor play to improved mental health, behaviour and resilience. Remember that we are talking about a brain that hasn't changed for millennia and that was never "built" to function indoors. Outdoor adventures are some of the richest sensory and exploratory experiences a child ever has and without them we are struggling as a species. Once again, working in a variety of settings I can see first-hand the difference between settings that truly embrace the outdoors and those that spend most of the day indoors.

Note on Forest Schools

I LOVE the Forest Schools community. It has done so much to promote outdoor play and raise awareness of the benefits of outdoor experiences. I recently delivered at a conference alongside Chris Dee who is the Director at Forest School Learning Initiative and she is so passionate about Forest Schools and amazing at persuading even parents who are not "outdoors" people to embrace being outdoors with their children. However, I am sure she wouldn't mind me saying that the outdoors existed long before Forest Schools teachers, so not having a Forest Schools qualification should never be a barrier to getting children outdoors. Please get a Forest Schools qualification if you can but don't stop children going outdoors if you can't. Also heart-breaking is when schools or nurseries have a wonderful "Forest School" that the children can use once a week. The rest of the time all they can do is gaze longingly into a wonderfully rich area they are not allowed to use unless it is Forest Schools time. I would always advise settings to get some form of Forest Schools training but please don't restrict children from going outside, not just for schooling or education but simply because of the incredible benefits of being outdoors.

There are also massive benefits to physical health from outdoor play and currently bone conditions such as rickets are increasing in the UK due to a simple lack of outdoor exposure. A significant amount of our vitamin D comes from sunlight so without it we are very likely to be deficient in this vital vitamin.

OK, I could probably go on about play deprivation symptoms all day, as to be honest, lack of play potentially impacts on every aspect of development and well-being. I will just finish, however, with a note on the brain. We are now moving into the realm of the chronically play-deprived child. This is not your children, not yet at any rate. This is what happens to a child when positive play experiences are completely absent from their life. In chronic play deprivation, there is a loss of electrical activity to parts of the brain and potentially a significant decrease in brain size. There is even some suggestion that play is so essential to brain growth that without it the brain does not grow to the correct shape and becomes malformed (Hughes, 2003). This is so catastrophic for our eventual well-being that it paints a very bleak picture of a future where play has declined at its current rate. Unfortunately, nobody, except for a few specialists, is talking about this as the global crisis it potentially could be. We need to take play deprivation seriously and do everything we can to balance embracing new technologies such as tablets and phones with the desperate need for children to have some good old-fashioned play.

7

PEOW, PEOW, PEOW, CLICK – PLAY AS POSITIVE BEHAVIOUR OR HOW TO SUPPORT CHILDREN TO FULFIL THEIR PLAY POTENTIAL

This book is not about behaviour. That would be a whole book in itself and I really want to make this book all about play, even though I clearly keep getting side-tracked (just don't mention magicians or cold compresses). However, Play, Curiosity and Nurturing are sometimes called pro-social emotions, which means they support pro-social behaviour. In my career, I have often been asked to work with children whose behaviour is considered challenging and the one thing I have repeatedly noticed is that children fully engaged in play do not exhibit anywhere near as much negative behaviour. I have already mentioned our sessions out in the woods with older children, some of whom have had severe, medically diagnosed behaviour conditions as well as extremely negative experiences of childhood. The truth is that some of these sessions have been really challenging but the benefits to the children and young people have been undeniable. Through providing positive play where the children feel safe, stimulated and valued, we have seen the most dramatic improvements in emotional well-being which has directly impacted on behaviour.

I don't think it is an exaggeration to say that play has been a key factor in promoting positive behaviour for every age of child we work with.

So, on that note and with this book definitely NOT being about behaviour, I just wanted to share one of the most useful and interesting theories I have ever encountered to do with play. If that theory just happens to coincidently be really significant for behaviour then that's just an added bonus.

A confession...

As a behaviour specialist working with young children, I came to a harsh realisation recently. This may be something you identify with (or it may be just me?) - I am much better at working with other people's children than my own! I often deliver positive behaviour training where the key points are looking at adult behaviour and how that directly impacts on our children. I then go home and catch myself saying or doing exactly the things I have just been teaching people not to do! I realise this makes me an enormous hypocrite, but it also points out that with the best will in the world we are only human. As parents, we will make many mistakes and are going to get it badly wrong sometimes. However, so long as we are trying to do the best for our children and make sure that their positive experiences of childhood outweigh the inevitable negatives, we are at least on the right track.

The best theory ever?

We are going to go back to our old friends Gordon Sturrock and Perry Else (1998), those legends of Playwork who gave us such lovely terms as "adulteration" and "dysplay". They came up with a unique and very simple way of describing the play process as it happens, called the "Play Cycle".

The Play Cycle is actually easier to experience than it is to describe, so I have a very quick task for you. I want you to pretend we are all young children and imagine what you would do if I ran up to you, pointed my fingers and said, *"Peow, peow, peow!"*?

Hey, why not actually do it? You won't look weird, I promise! Pretend to shoot the book; no one is judging you.

Some of you may have thought of shooting back, whilst others might have clutched their hearts and comedically expired. According to the Play Cycle, what I gave to you is called a "Play Cue": a simple act of initiating play – "Peow, peow, peow." You hopefully interpreted that Play Cue and gave me back a "Play Return" which would have been to continue the play by shooting back or pretending to die.

Once you are aware of these simple concepts, you begin to see Play Cues and Play Returns everywhere, constantly cycling through children's play. Hence the name, the Play Cycle.

At this point, I did not want to start a discussion on children playing with pretend guns, although it is an interesting and often controversial topic. I only chose that specific Play Cue because it is easily recognisable, even when described on a page. I could just as easily have run up to you and shouted "Tag!" before running away again. This would be another fairly straightforward Play Cue that you would have answered by chasing me. I could even verbalise my Play Cue and simply have asked, *"will you play with me?"*

Play Cues and Play Returns are fascinating to watch in our own children and something you can see first-hand whenever children play.

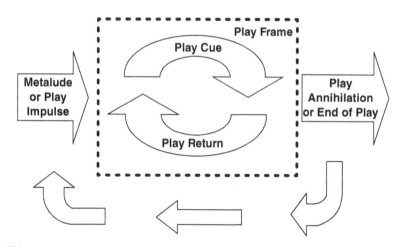

Figure 7.1

Source: Diagram adapted from Sturrock and Else (1998).

Unpicking the Play Cycle

Why is this significant for behaviour? Well, I never said it was because this book is about play, but if we did accidentally look at the Play Cycle from a neurological perspective there are huge (but entirely coincidental) implications for behaviour.

One aspect of the Play Cycle is the initial urge to play, sometimes called the "metalude", that precedes the Play Cue. Basically, this is the fundamental drive for play, the spark that starts the whole process. The interesting thing is that we now know where this urge or spark comes from. If we go back to Chapter 1 of this book and the work of Jaak Panksepp, we see that the "metalude" is not always a conscious decision and is just as likely to be an instinctive response from our primitive limbic system.

This means something really important about Play Cues. It means that there is no instruction manual or built-in guidance for what is, or isn't, an appropriate Play Cue. Children are not always conscious of their Play Cues and will instinctively do whatever is most developmentally appropriate, regardless of what that behaviour looks like to an adult. This sadly means that a significant number of Play Cues can be misinterpreted as negative behaviour. It is pretty much a case of whatever behaviour the limbic system instinctively comes up with, showing very little in the way of conscious thought.

If you are unsure of what this looks like, imagine now that you are all grown-ups. If I was a child and I ran up to you and then punched you, that would clearly be an unpleasant experience and seemingly an example of negative behaviour. If you were my parent at this point (which would be weird), I would probably receive a "telling off" with cross words and negative feelings all round.

What if, though, at that precise moment, my limbic system is steering me and urging me towards boisterous play? Boisterous play is not negative behaviour but a vital part of the developmental process. By hitting you, I have potentially just paid you one of the biggest compliments a child can ever pay an adult. I am emotionally secure enough with you to freely initiate play. This is NOT negative behaviour. This is a simple mistake made when expressing a vital system in the brain.

Now, I am not saying that we should accept being hit by our children. However, if we acknowledge that this is not in itself negative behaviour, but merely a flawed way of expressing the play urge, then our best strategy is to guide the child towards a more positive expression of their innate Play Cue, rather than making them feel like a criminal for something they had very little control over.

The joy of grass fighting...

One lovely example happened during a school lunchtime. A group of children and myself were engaging in a hearty grass fight with the mown grass left behind by the mower. There were squeals of joy and excitement throughout, but one girl was merely watching without joining in. I was just about to approach her to see if she wanted to play when she nervously walked towards me. She looked extremely uneasy to be talking to a visitor to the school and was clearly very anxious. I was expecting her to ask to play when instead she smiled and then stamped on my foot as hard as she could. It really hurt!

Any other member of staff in the school would have sent her to the Head for this behaviour. Stamping on a visitor's foot would probably have gained her all sorts of punishments and possibly a phone-call home. However, through the haze of pain I realised that this was probably a Play Cue. Yes, it was definitely a bad one and certainly not what I was expecting, but it did make a weird kind of sense. She had seen the joy, heard the laughter of the grass fight and wanted to join in. However, clearly underconfident and anxious she had built her courage up to the point where she was going to ask to play and then, in one terrible instinctive moment, had just got it badly wrong. Also remember that when we are anxious our decision-making capacity is impaired.

She knew she had got it wrong and looked at me with absolute horror and terror to the point where her neck actually disappeared as she shrank away from me in fear. She knew with complete certainty that the next thing to happen was she was going to be shouted at and/or sanctioned in some way. However, simply because of my knowledge of the Play Cycle I was able to ask, *"Did you do that because you wanted to play?"* She nodded, genuinely terrified at this point. *"Well, we are in luck,"* I continued, *"because I have a spare foot, so would you like to join in our grass fight?"* Once again, she nodded. Within 10 minutes, she was laughing and playing like all the other children.

There was no need for "discipline" or even in this case to make more than a cursory reference to the behaviour. She already knew exactly what she had done. Through steering her towards play, I not only helped her to engage in a positive, joyful experience but also, I believe, avoided a potentially catastrophic experience for her confidence and emotional well-being. All by simply being aware of Play Cues.

The girl in the previous example clearly knew that her behaviour was not appropriate (but only after she had done it). However, for many children, especially our younger ones, they often do not have the faintest clue that their Play Cue will be misinterpreted as negative behaviour. You have all encountered the child that does not know their own strength. You know, the one who shoves another child, and then looks surprised that there is a child-shaped hole in the wall?

Figure 7.2   Child-shaped hole drawn by PB

Now, obviously not every example of negative behaviour is a Play Cue "gone wrong", but you will now start to see that a significant number fall into that category. You will have to keep reminding and challenging children but my advice, if you think it is a misinterpreted Play Cue, is to handle it sensitively so that you can help guide the child towards play rather than restricting a 200,000-year-old instinct and raising anxiety at the same time.

Snot anyone?

My son, aged 4, wiped a bogey on me. Now I don't know about anybody else, but I really don't like snot. Working with children in nurseries, I always find it difficult to keep smiling when a child has snot hanging off their chin. How did they not notice it going over their lips? Eugh! But I digress. I was so appalled by my son that I had taken a deep breath in to shout at him. Then I saw his face. Grinning manically and devoid of anything resembling intelligence, just a boy with a bogey. Then it hit me (a thought not the bogey): children love icky things, bogeys are icky and so he wanted to play an icky, albeit mischievous game with his dad. This was a huge compliment which I would have completely missed without knowledge of the Play Cycle. Now I was still not happy about the whole bogey wiping thing, so I was very clear that I did not want him to do this again. However, instead of making him feel like a criminal, I told him I wasn't cross and if he promised to not wipe bogeys on me again, we could play an icky game that I knew. We then spent a disgusting 20 minutes playing "Beans or Spaghetti". This is a very simple sensory game involving guessing the difference between a bowl of tinned beans and a bowl of tinned spaghetti by squidging them, with your eyes shut (or blindfolded or behind your back, etc). As you have probably surmised, this is too easy for many children, so they have to use other body parts apart from their fingers. You do not know true horror until you have squidged beans with your toes! Regardless, no matter how disgusting this game is for adults, it was a wonderful and funny moment of father and son bonding which simply would not have happened if I had gone with my first instinct and shouted at him.

OK, so this is not replacing our existing behaviour strategies, just acknowledging that children's Play Cues can easily be misinterpreted. Once you start to observe Play Cues, you will soon see that a significant number of examples of so-called "negative behaviour" are actually simply misinterpreted Play Cues.

What happens when a child does not get returns for their cues?

The Play Cycle is significant for other reasons, though. Imagine now the child running around going, "Peow, peow, peow" and not getting any Play Returns. This is bound to happen quite frequently as not every child or adult wants to play with every other child or adult. A confident child will just go and give Play Cues to someone else. What if though, it is the same child, every time, not getting a Play Return? What if that child struggles to give Play Cues that another child or adult understands? What if a significant number of their Play Cues are misinterpreted as negative behaviour? I think we probably saw the outcomes for that child in the example with the grass fighting. A child who is very nervous and anxious about their Play Cues, probably exhibiting dysplay, is going to struggle to give appropriate Play Cues. If those cues are only infrequently returned, the child may stop giving Play Cues altogether, ultimately increasing their risk of play deprivation symptoms. This is a sad place for a child to find themselves in and if adults in their world do not pick up on these lost Play Cues, this could be catastrophic for the child's well-being. I think any adult who steps up and answers a Play Cue from a child that does not often get Play Returns is a genuine superhero. If we can be the one person, and it probably is just one person, who says, "Come on, let's play!" the effect on that child can be profound.

Just as an additional note: playworkers often firmly believe that an adult should never join in with children's play unless asked. There is a very good reason for this which is to stop adults taking over the play (adulteration) and making it all about them. Just be aware though that children don't always ask an adult to join in verbally and Play Cues can come in many different forms.

OK, so back to not talking about behaviour. What else can happen if a child's Play Cues are repeatedly ignored? Instead of withdrawing and limiting their expression of Play Cues, a child can do the opposite. Children will often escalate their Play Cues until they are now, to all intents and purposes, "negative behaviour".

"Peow, peow peow!" is clearly not working so the child picks up a chair and throws it instead. OK, so this may be an extreme example, but you will see instances of this kind of escalation quite frequently. One of the first lessons about behaviour (still not talking about behaviour) is that children will do what works. If a behaviour pattern, negative or positive, has the desired effect, they will repeat that behaviour. If ordinary Play Cues are being ignored, it is very likely that you will see negative behaviour, simply as a way to fulfil these vital urges in the child's brain.

Not now, I'm busy...

OK, the last word about my son. He is actually a really great child and would be mortified that I am using him as an example of negative behaviour. However, when he was very young, he went for the classic Play Cue, *"Daddy, will you play with me?"* whilst tugging at my clothes. Old school! Unfortunately, at this point I was hard at work writing an email and had to say, *"I'll play with you in five minutes".* Even though this is not in itself bad, as we can't play with our children all the time, the problem is that when an adult says five minutes, it very rarely is five minutes. So, twenty minutes pass (an eon to a 4-year-old) and he is tugging on my clothes more insistently: *"Daddy, you said you would play with me?"* This time I don't reply in quite such a friendly way: *"I know I said I would play with you but Daddy's work is important".* I turned round a few minutes later and he was breaking a plastic guitar on his sister's head. (True story and explains why my daughter is innately talented at music but also has a flat head.)

It is easy to see in hindsight what had happened. I had ignored several positive Play Cues and because they had not worked my son escalated to negative behaviour. Being made to wait for what was, to a child, an unfeasibly long time would also have been a factor in raising his anxiety and frustration levels, and ultimately leading to negative behaviour.

I believe the Play Cycle and its ramifications are one of the most useful theories ever created. There is much more to it than I have the time to do justice, but I wanted readers to have something tangible they can observe in their own children of any age. Even more amazing is that I managed to get through this chapter without mentioning behaviour once!

· ·

Reflective Questions

Simply observe children and look out for Play Cues:

Are those cues mistaken for negative behaviour?

Do those Play Cues go unnoticed by other children?

Do children want us to play?

Are there children in our setting who struggle with Play Cues?

What can we do to support the Play Cycle?

· ·

Chapter Summary

As parents, we can't play with our children all the time. However, knowing how important play is, and recognising the instinctive nature of Play Cues, can have a huge impact on the whole family. It certainly has had for us. For some families, the simple recognition that the child is not "deliberately" misbehaving but is simply wanting to play can make a huge difference to how we interact with our children positively.

If we work in any setting with children of any age, this theory is phenomenally useful for creating a positive, playful atmosphere for our children. Also, by recognising the limitations of the limbic system and the Play Cues the child instinctively gives, we can be a little bit more tolerant of children's behaviour and better equipped to guide children towards positive expressions of the fundamental urge to play.

8

HOW DID YOU USED TO PLAY, GRANDMA? – PLAY FOR THE FUTURE OF HUMANITY

Remember that right at the very beginning we talked about the lady rat that preferred to mate with rats who had experienced lots of play? This suggests that play is not merely beneficial for the current generation but is also a behavioural trait to be preserved for future generations. It also suggests that the playful behaviours we experience now can in some way affect future generations. Surely this is nonsense?

My understanding of genetics is sketchy at best. I vividly remember facts that are of relevance to my life but pretty much forget everything else. It may be my ADHD or just normal human behaviour, but I can tell you the names of parts of the brain significant for children developing empathy (anterior cingulate cortex for one) but can't tell you a single thing about gardening. Genetics just never seemed to have any relevance to me because I can't affect or impact on a child's genetics one way or the other.

So, for those who need a refresher in genetics, here goes. When a woman and a man love each other very much, they share a special cuddle and they have a baby. The baby's physical attributes (eye colour, height, hair colour) are dictated by the genetic material from the two parents. The blueprint for the child's body is in the DNA which is combined from the two parents.

This never seemed that important to me because there is no way even the best childcare workers can affect the fundamental DNA of a child. I firmly believed that a child's DNA was set in stone and unless we are actually present at the conception (which could be awkward) then we can't alter or affect the genetic code of a child in any way, no matter how good we are at our job.

The truth is, I was completely wrong.

The study of epigenetics, which is a relatively new branch of genetics, tells us something utterly remarkable. Your genes are not set in stone. Childhood experiences can switch on and off genetic markers in the DNA and pass that on to the next generation. This is one of the most mind-blowing and significant things I have ever learned in 30 years of working with children. When children experience positive, stimulating and playful environments, full of nurturing and wonderful interactions, they begin to change their DNA. One example is that those positive experiences switch off the DNA markers for high-stress factor responses such as cortisol production. This genetic change is then passed on to the next generation, making them less susceptible to stress, better able to cope with anxiety and with better prospects for mental health and emotional well-being.

Just think about what this means for a moment. This means that the next time you work with children, or interact positively with your own children, and you give them wonderful childhood experiences full of Play, Curiosity and Nurturing, you are not just benefitting that child potentially for the rest of their life. You are also affecting the life chances and emotional well-being of their future unborn children by altering that child's fundamental DNA. This means that the impact of our positive interactions with children will be felt not just throughout the child's lifetime but for the next generation. I don't know about anyone else, but I find this both humbling and amazing at the same time.

This means that working with children is more significant than we could have ever dreamed, shaping not just the children themselves but future generations of children, children we may never even meet but have helped nonetheless.

Investing in children

Studies such as this show us a fundamental truth about our world. If we want it to be a better place, we need to invest in children. There are no longer any excuses to hide behind. The neuroscience, biochemistry and epigenetics of childhood show us unambiguously what we need to do, right now, to ensure a better future for our species.

We know, for instance, that the most significant amount of brain growth happens in early years – so this is the most important time for a child's development – not secondary school or university but nursery settings and homes. This is where investment needs to go to give every child a chance of reaching their full brain growth potential. We know that play is a key brain growth process, producing BDNF which actively speeds up brain growth. Yet play as a discipline is almost universally undervalued. Adults facilitating play for their children should be paid the same as a secondary school teacher because their level of influence on a child's development and emotional well-being is just as significant, if not more so.

We also know that adult health, both physical and mental, is intrinsically linked to early childhood. If we want a healthy society, we need to invest in early childhood rather than waiting until the ever-decreasing health of our populations reaches crisis point. Children build the strong healthy bodies and minds they need in adulthood through play. We need to make sure every single child gets opportunities to experience a broad range of positive play to ensure they stay as healthy and emotionally secure as possible throughout their adult life.

And if none of that is convincing you – if you think that the current state of affairs is acceptable because spending money on early childhood is low on the list of priorities for a nation wanting to be prosperous and economically viable, think again. Investing in children yields one of the highest returns of investment of any aspect of a nation's economy. Studies by the Heckman Institute show that investing in early childhood actually increases the wealth of a country, increasing the social mobility of even its poorest citizens and boosting the overall economy by a hugely significant amount (Gertler et al, 2014).

Children already know that play is great but are very unlikely to be heard in a society that doesn't always value play. If we don't stand up for children's right to play, then the chances are that no one else will. It is no longer enough to know about the benefits of play. It is not even enough to provide amazing play opportunities for our children. We also need to stand up and shout about play and make sure that as many people as possible understand this essential process.

Article 31 of the UN Convention on the Rights of a Child (1989) states that every child has a fundamental right to play.

So, the next time someone tells you play is frivolous or complains that children need to be doing something more important, you now know exactly what to tell them. Play is not just important, it is essential. It is not just good for children; it is profound and life-changing. It may sometimes look frivolous, but it is building the brains, bones, bodies, hearts, lungs, well-being, confidence, problem solving, imagination, academic skills, creativity, mental health and even life expectancy of our children. From neuroscience and evolutionary biology to biochemistry and epigenetics, play is potentially the most important thing children will ever do. It is the difference between children struggling with life and children thriving, and quite literally a matter of life and death.

The final word on magicians

During one of our adoption sessions, a child had convinced a potential adopter to sit on a scooter-board with him and race down a concrete path. The path was quite steep and I was nervous about the whole thing. However, I quickly assessed the risk and benefit and realised that sitting on the adopter's lap, experiencing excitement and fun was a benefit that outweighed the potential risk of falling off. OK, so they fell off. The child was crying and holding his bruised knee, but the adopter was holding him and comforting him in a moment of shared experience, bonding and nurturing. The child was just beginning to relax because he felt so safe in the arms of this adopter when up walked the magician. He took the child off the adopter and proceeded to apply, yes, you've guessed it, a cold compress, to the child's knee. My worst nightmare had come true - a magician with a cold compress!

Interestingly, when these events get televised, my teams (including myself) never feature very prominently in the footage. We are always there in the background just doing our job, making sure the children have a wonderful, playful time. This is fine and just as it should be; the events (and the documentaries) are about children after all. I'll tell you who does often feature quite prominently though, the magicians. Magicians are entertaining and vibrant, often charismatic and wearing funny outfits, so naturally they make good television. We are a little bit scruffy, covered in mud, paint, glitter (and often snot), and just not all that show biz. Realistically, it makes perfect sense that we are in the background.

I mentioned this fact on social media once and I am worried I came across as a bitter old man. The truth is I am not bitter about this; I understand how the magicians of the world will obviously get the attention because, let's be honest, they look a lot more interesting than us. I don't think things are going to change in my lifetime. I think as a person who works with children I am always going to be undervalued, just as we all are, when compared to business types, scientists, politicians and yes even magicians. I am never going to be paid as much as a film star or footballer. But at least now I know the truth.

No magician ever had such a profound impact on children as an early years worker or playworker. Some humans change the world when they come up with a new theory or invention. We change the world every time we work with children. There are no perks to our work except the knowledge that we are, child by child, making the world a better place.

The future

You might also like to know that studies in epigenetics show that the positive genetic effect is not about just one generation, but two. So, the next time you work with children, you are not just profoundly affecting that child, but also improving the potential for emotional well-being for their unborn children, *and* their unborn grandchildren.

This means something quite simple. If every government in every country in the world invested in children so that every child in the world experienced Play, Curiosity and Nurturing with caring adults full of compassion and joy, within two generations our entire species would have changed for the better. As a species, we would be less war-like, more empathic, with better mental health, less anti-social behaviour, less anxiety and better prospects for life-long emotional well-being. Our entire species could be changed at the genetic level to be better. All because of investing in Play, Curiosity and Nurturing.

So, would you rather wear a sequined waistcoat, earn lots of money and be recognised on TV? Or would you rather fundamentally change the human race every time you work with children?

Pick a card, any card? (Only kidding.)

The end! (Or hopefully only the beginning of a better world through play.)

APPENDIX

Letter to parents from settings

This is a standard letter we send out to parents of our projects. Please feel free to use, edit and amend this.

Dear Parent,

We are fully committed to giving our children a high quality play experience and understand the importance of play to children's development. Play can have a profound effect on children's confidence, self-esteem and mental and physical health and has been proven to be an essential element in healthy brain development. Recent studies have shown that play is potentially the most important developmental process in any child's life.

- Play can be messy. Because of the enormous benefits of messy play, we encourage children to do activities where they may get muddy, dirty or messy. Exploring sensory and messy play builds neural networks in a child's brain that underpin problem solving, creativity and imagination. Please don't bring them to nursery/school in expensive clothing.

- Children are waterproof. Lack of outdoor play can be extremely bad for children's health and has recently been linked to an increase in rickets in the UK. There are also several studies linking outdoor play to improved behaviour and mental health as well as promoting healthy eyesight. We will play outside in all weathers so please ensure your child has suitable clothing for outdoor play, even if they arrive at nursery/school by car.

- We are committed to protecting children from serious harm but we also believe that minor bumps and bruises are an important part of growing up. You only have to think back to your own childhoods to know this is true. We will sometimes play games where the occasional bump and bruise is possible because of the enormous benefits these experiences have on the development and well-being of children. Studies have shown that over-protecting children can harm their development and that experiencing controlled risk through play can better prepare them for real-life risk.

- We believe that we are harming children's resilience if we continue to treat insignificant injuries. We will use a common-sense approach to assess which injuries genuinely need attention and those which the child can better deal with by continuing playing. Children with minor bruises will be gently encouraged to carry on playing (just like we all did when we were children) rather than taking up time that could be better spent helping children play. This will help children become more physically and emotionally resilient.

Please sign below to indicate that you have read and understood our commitment to play and we hope you will support us in making play as exciting and fun as possible at a time when many children are not getting sufficient quality play in their lives.

Signed _____Date_____

REFERENCES AND FURTHER READING

Ball, D., Gill, T. and Spiegal, B. (2008) *Managing Risk in Play Provision: Implementation Guide*. London: DCSF.

Biven, L. and Panksepp, J. (2012) *The Archaeology of Mind: Neuroevolutionary Origins of Human Emotion*. London: W.W. Norton & Co.

Botterill, G. (2018) *Can I Go and Play Now? Rethinking the Early Years*. London: Sage.

Brown, F. (2003) *Playwork: Theory and Practice*. Buckingham: Open University Press.

Gascoyne, S. (2018) *Messy Play in the Early Years*. Abingdon: Routledge.

Gertler, P., Heckman, J., Pinto, R., Zanolini, A., Vermeersch, C., Walker, S., Chang, S.M. and Grantham-McGregor, S. (2014) 'Labor market returns to an early childhood stimulation intervention in Jamaica', *Science*, 30;344(6187): 998-1001.

Goddard Blythe, S. (2018) *Movement: Your Child's First Language (Early Years): How Music and Movement Assist Brain Development in Children Aged 3-7 Years*. Stroud: Hawthorn Press.

Hughes, B. (2002) *A Playworker's Taxonomy of Play Types*. London: Playlink.

Hughes, B. (2003) *Play Deprivation - Facts and Interpretations*. Play Wales.

Lieberman, J. N. (2014) *Playfulness: Its Relationship to Imagination and Creativity*. Cambridge, MA: Academic Press.

National Scientific Council on the Developing Child (2010) Early Experiences Can Alter Gene Expression and Affect Long-Term Development. Working Paper No. 10.

Newman, R. (2017) *Neuropolis: A Brain Science Survival Guide*. London: William Collins.

Nicholson, S. (1971) 'How NOT to cheat children - The Theory of Loose Parts', *Landscape Architecture*, Volume 62.

Panksepp, J. and Biven, L. (2012) *The Archaeology of Mind: Neuroevolutionary Origins of Human Emotion*. New York: W. W. Norton & Co.

Play England (2011) A world without play: An expert view.

Schlegel, A., Kohler, P.J., Fogelson, S.V., Alexander, P., Konuthula, D. and Tse, P.U. (2013) 'Network structure and dynamics of the mental workspace', *Proceedings of the National Academy of Sciences of the United States of America*, 1;110(40): 16277–82.

Sturrock, G. and Else, P. (1998) *'The Colorado Paper' – The playground as therapeutic space: playwork as healing. In Play in a changing society: Research, design, application.* The IPA/USA triennial national conference. June 1998.

Sunderland, M. (2007) *What Every Parent Needs To Know: Love, Nurture and Play with Your Child.* London: Dorling Kindersley.

The United Nations Convention on the Rights of the Child (1989).

World Economic Forum (2022) 5 Things to Know About the Future of Jobs. Retreived from https://www.weforum.org/agenda/2018/09/future-of-jobs-2018-things-to-know/

INDEX